The Relentless Search for *Better Ways*

The Relentless Search for Better Ways

*Happily Ever Afters
Don't Just Happen*

Jim Bearden, CSP

HEA Publishing

Austin, Texas

Copyright © 2007 by Jim Bearden, CSP

All rights reserved.
No part of this book may be reproduced or utilized in any form
or by any means, electronic or mechanical, including
photocopying, recording or by any information storage
and retrieval system, without permission
in writing from the Publisher.

Inquiries should be addressed to
P. O. Box 161902
Austin, Texas 78716

First Edition
First Printing 2006
Second Printing 2007
Third Printing 2009

www.jimbearden.com

Library of Congress Card Number 2006921559

ISBN 0-9777049-0-4

Printed in the United States of America

To Barbara

*Together we've dreamed, and together we've worked
to make our dreams come true.
In case you haven't noticed,
I have relied on your strength,
your love and your faith
whenever we've hit a bump in the road.
We simply would not be
where we are if it weren't for you.*

In my life, you are *the dream,
and I still can't believe you came true.*

Table of Contents

Introduction xiii

Chapter 1
Three Boys, Some Beer—and a Cop 1

Chapter 2
The "Happily Ever After" Myth 12

Chapter 3
From Victimhood to Accountability 31

Chapter 4
Change-Friendly Cultures 70

Chapter 5
Participants in the Search for Better Ways 93

Chapter 6
Searching for Better Ways 112

Chapter 7
Continuous Process Improvement 145

Chapter 8
Leadership 161

Chapter 9
How Winning Occurs—In the Real World 180

Preface

Don't you just love a good story? Given the choice between sitting through a lecture and hearing some stories, I'll pick the stories every time. In fact, that's the choice I've made about my life's work.

As a professional speaker, I have used stories to illustrate concepts like accountability, leadership and winning. My presentations on topics related to individual and organizational success are filled with stores about real-world experiences; mostly mine. And most of them are humorous.

While I am convinced that the topics I cover in my keynote presentations, seminars and workshops are important ones, my approach to them is light-hearted. If we can laugh—or at least smile—about things we're doing, we'll probably be willing to consider alternatives. Laughing and learning seem to go hand-in-hand.

I've taken that very same approach in this book. My writing style reflects my speaking style. Translate that to mean lots of stories. I hope my stories will work as well for you, the reader, as they have over the past nineteen years for the audiences who have heard me tell them. I also hope they make you smile.

Enough about my writing style. Let me tell you about my book.

This is a book about winning in the real world. It is a book for people interested in more than just ideas or concepts about winning. It is a book about doing, about choices made and the consequences of those choices. It is a book for people whose success—in any area of their lives—is measured by the choices other people make. It is intended for people whose individual success impacts—and is impacted by—the success of the organizations with which they're associated. It is a book for people whose success is determined by their ability to influence the choices others make.

It is a book for people who are willing to do more than just read. It is a book for people who are ready to move beyond theory and do some practical learning.

Practical learning is the process of converting theories (ideas) into practice (action), and I have been blessed with many opportunities to do just that. Two of those experiences, and the roles I played, provided me with many of the lessons and insights I'll share with you.

During 1968 and 1969 I served as a Marine rifle platoon and rifle company commander in Vietnam. One afternoon in July 1968, the theoretical phase of my Marine training ended and the practical phase began—with a bang! The ensuing thirteen-month tour of duty was the crucible in which my ability to translate theory into practice was tested and refined. What emerged were real-world insights on organizational dynamics and cultures, continuous process improvement, collaborative processes, personal accountability, and leadership.

In the years since then, I have found those insights and lessons relevant to every organization in which I've worked and to the roles I've played in those organizations. Those insights and lessons are prominently featured in this book.

Beginning in 1976, and continuing to this very day, I have served as a father. Early on the morning of March 1, 1976, the theoretical phase of my "Daddy" training ended and the practical phase began—with a wail. Ryan Matthew Bearden, the first of my three children, came into the world eager to function as one of my most valuable and relentless teachers.

On June 29, 1989, Ryan was joined by a sister, Annie Stone Bearden. And the two of them helped us greet the third and final member of our trio on November 22, 1991, when Jessica Maxwell Bearden joined the fold. I'm convinced that the Lord decided that since I'd learned so much from my first teacher, Ryan, he'd give me two more. And just to make sure that my "Daddy" learning was complete, he made both of them girls.

My thirty years as a father and the experiences I've had with my children and my wife, Barbara, during those years, have convinced me that the home is the cradle of all learning. The lessons learned in the home, in my role as father and husband, are also relevant to other organizational settings and to the roles people play in those settings. Organizational dynamics and cultures, continuous process improvement, collaborative processes, personal accountability, and leadership are important in the home, the workplace, the classroom, the church, the association, the practice, and the community.

In the real world, winning is a process, not an event. In organizational settings, it is a composite of the choices individuals make and the consequences of those choices. To improve the quality of the consequences, we must be willing to acknowledge and improve the quality of the choices we make.

In the real world, the people, situations and circumstances in our lives change, and as they change, so do the requirements for our success. That applies to individuals and to organizations. In order to keep pace with the changes encountered and to meet the changing requirements for their success, organizations must make changes. Process improvement is not discretionary. But, as we all know, it isn't the organizations that make changes; it's the people within those organizations. Process improvement is a people-driven dynamic.

This is a book about organizational success, about winning in organizational settings. It is a book for all the people whose efforts are required for such success. That would include the people responsible for facilitating process improvement and the people whose sustained efforts are required for implementing new processes.

Finally, this is a book about individual and organizational accountability. It is a book for people who are ready and willing to acknowledge their ownership of the choices they make and of the consequences those choices produce. In the real world, winning—or sustained progress—without accountability, just won't happen.

And that's the real lesson I'm learning and the one I'm seeking to impart in this book. When other people's lives are impacted by the choices we make, we're not just remiss if we refuse to acknowledge and try to improve those choices, we're personally and professionally irresponsible. The learning that started to take shape long ago on a hill in Vietnam, and the lessons that have been reinforced continuously over the past thirty years in my home and many other settings have formed the basis of my requirements for winning. They are the lessons I'll share with you in this book.

This is a book about winning.

Jim Bearden
Austin, Texas

INTRODUCTION

As a novice golfer, I'm always on the lookout for any indication of progress. Trust me, they're few and far between, so when I discover such "evidence," I can't wait to share it. Remember, I'm a speaker and a writer. Sharing is what I do.

I recently described to my mother-in-law a particularly good round I'd just completed, as she herself is an accomplished golfer. I also mentioned one or two things I could have done differently and my conviction that, had I done so, my score would have been lower.

My mother-in-law responded by telling me that I was becoming a "typical golfer," as evidenced by my use of "should'ves," "could'ves," and "would'ves." This little exchange was characteristic of my most valuable learning experiences, in which I've been forced to look back on my actions and reevaluate them. I'm fortunate to have been blessed with many rich life experiences that have provided me with excellent, if sometimes difficult, opportunities to learn valuable lessons.

Have I always learned from those experiences? No, but I have discovered that opportunities to learn and relearn potentially valuable lessons abound. If I don't pick up the clues or cues from one exposure, I can be sure that I will be presented with plenty of other opportunities to do so.

Choice and Consequences

What I will do in this book is share my thoughts on the process of achieving success—winning—both as an individual and on an organizational level. Specifically, I'll return again and again to the relationship between the choices we make and the consequences of those choices, how they impact the quality of our relationships, our work, our play—our lives. In doing so, I will rely heavily on my own life experiences and the conclusions I've drawn, the lessons I've learned from them.

As you read about my experiences, I invite you to reflect on the people, events, and circumstances you've encountered in your life experiences. While they will differ from mine, I'm guessing there will be more than a few similarities, as well as variations on the lessons I've learned. I encourage you to let my stories take you back to the learning opportunities you've had and to extract from them the lessons they held for you. Compare your lessons to the ones I'll describe, and then, create your own.

Finally, I invite you to do what I've begun doing, and that is to start looking for the lessons in your everyday life experiences. Here's what I'm discovering: The more willing I am to step back from events and look for the lessons they might contain, the more likely I am to find those lessons. The more actively we look for something, assuming we're looking in the right places, the better chance we have of finding it.

This process of looking for lessons has had the added benefit of helping me determine how to apply those lessons. As I look for those lessons in my experiences with people, situations, and circumstances, I find that my effectiveness at dealing with them improves. I'm able to disengage my "autopilot" and look for better ways of doing things. That's really the theme of this book, what I call the Relentless Search for Better Ways. That search begins when you start paying attention to the experiences that reveal a need for changing the status quo.

So that's how I'll begin, with just such an experience, a story that I call "Three Boys, Some Beer—and a Cop."

Chapter 1

Three Boys, Some Beer— and a Cop

My upbringing in West Texas, my time as a Marine, my work, and my exploits on the golf course are all topics you'll hear more—much more—about. But the setting in which I've learned the most is my home, and the role that has proven the most challenging and rewarding has been my role as a dad. My children would quickly verify that I have often needed to find "better ways."

Most people, especially parents, will agree that the home is a great setting for both learning and teaching. It seems to me, though, that one mistake we've often made is in not realizing who's really teaching whom. We've always accepted the notion that the tall ones are the teachers and the short ones are the students. I agree that such is the case most of the time.

However, I've also discovered that if we pay attention, we big ones can learn a lot from those little ones. And as with life itself, if we don't pay attention, those persistent little ones will continue trying to teach us the lessons we so need to learn. Surely one reason little kids cry so much is out of frustration with having to deal with us slow learners who are so much bigger than they are.

Back to my experience. It involved the oldest of my three children, my son Ryan. In fact, let me introduce you to the family right now. My wife is the "sainted" Barbara, and my children are Ryan, age thirty as of this writing; Annie, sixteen; and Jessie, fourteen.

Where was I? Oh yeah, the boys. This event occurred in 1990, on a Friday night between the hours of nine and eleven. Not bad recall for an old guy, right? I know it was 1990 because that was the year—one that will live in infamy—that Ryan turned sixteen and became a licensed driver. I know it was a Friday night because he was out on the town with two of his best buddies, who were also recently licensed drivers. I know it was after nine o'clock, because I was asleep.

Let me stop here and remind all of you of something you already know: time passes much faster when you're asleep than when you're awake. When Ryan and his buddies were out amazing themselves with all the discoveries that come with being teenage males, I found that I could make the time go faster by simply going to sleep. Best I can recall, I slept quite a bit for several years.

I know it was before eleven o'clock because Ryan wasn't home yet. Trust me, there was no way he'd be home before his curfew. So there you have the scenario. I was asleep in my bed when Barbara shook me awake and informed me that someone was knocking at the front door.

When that bit of news got through to my brain—which had just been rudely snatched from the sleep state—I got up and headed downstairs to investigate. When I got to the bottom of the stairs, I could see our front door, which had a large glass window. Through that glass I saw, standing on my front porch, an adult male wearing a windbreaker with one word emblazoned across its front. And what was that word? Why naturally, it was "Police."

Parents, what do you think went through my mind when I saw this? What sort of images did I conjure up? Trust me, I was not thinking that a police officer on my porch at that hour was there to deliver good news. In fact, I was terrified. My mind kicked into high gear and began cranking out images of Ryan injured, or worse. All I could think was, "Oh my God! Something's happened to Ryan," and I immediately began doing what any parent would do under those circumstances: I started making promises to the Almighty. I'm sure you parents can identify with my eagerness to strike a bargain with the Lord. I mean, I was doing my best negotiating, saying things like, "If you'll let him be OK, I'll never do [fill in the blank] again. No more of this Sunday morning golf. No sir, I'm on the front row, Sir." And you could almost hear him up there checking these things off.

I walked toward the front door, not really wanting to get there, not wanting to hear what I was afraid I was going to hear. But as I got closer, I saw, standing back in the shadows looking like he might be ready to strike a deal with the Almighty himself, my son, Ryan Matthew. The wave of relief I experienced upon seeing him was quickly replaced by another sentiment, one familiar to fathers everywhere. My recent promises to the Lord notwithstanding, I recovered my sense of duty and firmly swore that as soon as the officer left, I would kill Ryan, kill him with my own bare hands.

But first I had to get past the cop. So I opened the door, and the officer explained the nature of Ryan's indiscretion. Seems that Ryan and one of his two buddies had been apprehended while engaged in criminal activity. Oh, the humiliation I felt when the officer disclosed that, between the two of them, Ryan and his buddy had consumed approximately two beers! Apparently it was difficult to assess the exact amount consumed, given the boys' haste to dispose of the evidence when faced with imminent arrest.

The officer then broke the good news and told me, "In this jurisdiction, Mr. Bearden, our policy on underage drinking is that unless they're engaged in some other form of criminal activity, we don't arrest them, we bring them home and turn them over to their parents." Pause here for a moment and reflect on the way this news was greeted by the two Bearden "boys" involved. I was nearly ecstatic; Ryan, semi-suicidal. In retrospect, I've tried to put myself in Ryan's place. And I can tell you without reservation, that given a choice between being thrown into a drunk tank with the vilest of specimens and being turned over to my own father, I would have gladly—giddily—taken the tank.

I told the officer that this was an example of good public policy. I assured him that if he would simply turn the guilty lad over to me, justice would be done. At this point, Ryan slinked by me into the house, doing one of those "walking hunkers," and I started to close the door so I could attend to my fatherly duty—killing Ryan.

But the officer wasn't through. I'm guessing he hadn't often been so appreciated for bearing what was less than great news, so he decided to take me into his confidence about something Ryan had said while being transported to his doom. He asked me to step out on the porch, where he offered to tell me "something funny that happened." Needless to say, the man had his work cut out for him, because so far nothing he had said had been particularly amusing. Fearing that he would recognize my homicidal tendencies toward Ryan and take him into protective custody, I decided to humor him. The officer said that as he pulled into our driveway, Ryan—in a flash of brilliance—had leaned toward the front and said, "Officer, you can just let me off here, and I'll walk the rest of the way." Boy's quick, isn't he? It didn't work.

The Silver Lining

This event, when viewed from a parental perspective, displays every symptom of a setback, something of a problem, right? It easily qualified as an event that I would have happily missed out on. However, it also provided me with at least a couple of opportunities. On one hand, it gave me pretty much carte blanche to mete out "justice." Based on my well-honed parenting skills, all learned "on the job" with Ryan, that's the path I was accustomed to taking. Would I really have killed him? Of course not, but I would have made it abundantly clear that murder wasn't too far outside the realm of possibility.

But here's the revelation this event yielded upon closer examination. It provided me with an excellent, but difficult, opportunity to take a look at how I was parenting Ryan. It also revealed a lot about the impact of my parenting on our relationship, and on my ability to influence his choices.

Before I go any further, I should point out that Ryan has turned out to be the best man I've known in my life. He's always been a better son than I've been a dad, and I'm eternally thankful for him and how his presence has blessed my life and the lives of everyone he's ever touched.

But back to the event. It gave me an opportunity to step back and take a look at how I had communicated with Ryan and to consider the possibility that there just might be room for improvement. That should not come as much of a surprise, given the fact that we parents
don't take courses in parenting before we find ourselves in that role. Parenting is pretty much learned on the job, and when do we start developing those skills? When our children are small. Unfortunately, many of the skills learned when they're infants, or even young adolescents, may prove ineffective as our children grow up. Even more unfortunately, skills learned back then may

have become habits—and we know how difficult it is to break a habit.

This event was a gold mine of learning opportunities. Happily, I tapped into those opportunities immediately after the "arrest" and many times since then. The lessons of this experience form the theme of this book.

Change Isn't Optional

The first lesson of this experience with Ryan was a true epiphany for me:

> **The people, situations, and circumstances in our lives change.
> They always have, and they always will.**

In this situation, Ryan was the one who had changed. The little rascal had grown up. I know, you're thinking I surely do have an uncanny grasp of the obvious; of course he was growing up. That's what small people do. But you must also concede that the closer we are to something that is changing bit by bit over a long period of time, the more oblivious we can be to the implications of those changes. I could see that he was getting larger, and I could certainly recognize that his perception of me was changing. I was becoming a blithering idiot, right before his eyes. What escaped my notice was how his changes would create the need for me to make changes.

The second lesson, and probably the more important of these first two, was that:

> **As the people, situations & circumstances in our lives change, so do the requirements for our success.**

In order to deal effectively with the changes Ryan was experiencing, I would need to change the way I parented, especially the way I communicated with him. It's not enough just to acknowledge changes in the people, situations, and circumstances in our lives. We must also determine the impact those changes will have on us and what we must do in order to deal effectively with them.

Change and Organizations

This same phenomenon occurs in every organizational setting as well. For example, your customers, staff, managers, vendors, patients, and all your other constituencies will change—frequently and continuously. Their expectations, needs and priorities, likes and dislikes, and moods will all change. And as those changes manifest themselves, the requirements for your success with those people will also change.

Ryan had changed physically, but even more importantly, he had changed in terms of his ability to make choices. At sixteen he had options that weren't available to him when he was little, and the consequences of the choices he could make at sixteen had become more significant. At sixteen, the choices he made could potentially have fatal consequences. The requirements for my success as a parent had changed dramatically. I recognized that this event had given me an opportunity to take a hard look at the choices I had made, and was making, as a parent. It also revealed to me the impact my choices were having on Ryan's choices. I realized that I had to get over the notion that I had control over him and come to terms with the fact that the very best I can ever do is influence the choices he makes.

That same fact applies to you and all the people whose cooperation is essential to your success. Dealing effectively with the changes in those people, as well as the changing situations and circumstances you encounter, will require you to make regular changes in what you do and how you do it. It's all part of the Relentless Search for Better Ways.

My experience with Ryan provided an opportunity for me to acknowledge the relationship between the changes we encounter, the impact of those changes on the requirements for our continued success, and the need for us to make changes. As you might suspect, my experiences in the workplace have reinforced those important lessons, and one of those experiences was especially educational.

Selling Radio: The Early Years

If I had gone looking for a job that provided me with learning opportunities, I'm not sure that I could have found one that was better than sales. And the intangible service I was selling compounded the learning opportunities. Did I see them as opportunities then? No. In fact, I tended to lump them into one of two categories: agony or ecstasy.

In the world of radio, ratings matter—a lot. Four times each year, radio station listeners are selected at random and asked to keep diaries of their listening habits. They identify the stations they listen to, the times at which they listen, and the length of time for which they do so. All very scientific, I guess. What that means is that there is the potential for changes in the ratings four times each year. And as the ratings change, so do the requirements for radio salespeople's success.

There are essentially two categories of clients for radio advertising. First, there are the direct clients, usually the smaller, locally owned businesses, whose owners or managers place their own advertising. Other clients, usually the larger companies, are represented by advertising agencies. In advertising agencies, media experts decide which stations to use. While clients in both categories might be aware of a station's current ratings, the agency media buyers place far more emphasis on them than do most direct clients. As a station's ratings go up, media buyers are far more inclined to advertise on that station. And when they go down? Well, you might have trouble even making an appointment with them.

As the ratings circumstances changed, so did the requirements for my success as a radio sales rep. When they were high, agency media buyers often called in to place orders, without my having to do much in the way of selling. Getting bought is a whole lot easier than selling, but it's also a circumstantial phenomenon. And sure enough, our ratings went down. Way down.

At that point I had a couple of options. I could have waited for ratings to go back up, hoping that they would do so before my family and I starved. Or, I could have shifted my focus to prospects and clients who were not so enamored with ratings. With much encouragement from my sales manager and my family, I chose that second option. Trust me, getting bought was great while it lasted, but like most arrangements that are dependent on specific circumstances, it didn't last. The circumstances changed, and as they did, so did the requirements for my success as a salesperson. Here's an important takeaway from this experience:

> **The potential for success does not disappear just because the requirements for success have changed.**

The extent to which our success depends on our effectiveness with people is the extent to which we must be willing to acknowledge and improve the way we deal with them. Put another way:

> **Before we can expect to effectively influence the choices others make, we must be willing to acknowledge and improve the choices we make.**

We can start improving the choices we make by acknowledging the distinction between the Relentless Search for Better Ways and the frantic, but futile, search for Happily Ever Afters.

Chapter 1 Summary

- The people, situations and circumstances in our lives change.

- As the people, situations and circumstances in our lives change, so do the requirements for our success.

- The potential for success does not disappear just because the requirements for success have changed.

- In order to satisfy the changing requirements for their success, individuals and organizations must engage in a Relentless Search for Better Ways.

- If our success is impacted by the choices other people make, we must be willing to acknowledge and improve the ways we interact with those people.

- Before we can expect to effectively influence the choices others make, we must be willing to acknowledge and improve the choices we make.

Chapter 2

The "Happily Ever After" Myth

Throughout this book, I'll make references to quality of life. Feelings or emotions are the standards I use for assessing that quality. Obviously, happiness is a desirable feeling and a good standard for measuring quality of life.

The problem most of us seem to have with happiness nowadays is confusion about cause and effect:

> **Somehow we've reached the conclusion
> that happiness is an effect,
> the result of something that takes place in our lives.**

In short, we operate with the belief that outside phenomena, e.g., the people, situations, events, and circumstances we encounter cause us to be happy or unhappy. Being rational enough to prefer happiness over unhappiness, we avoid the things we are convinced will "make us" unhappy. We actively—even frantically—seek out the things we believe will make us happy, and not just temporarily, but for "ever after."

So where did we come up with the notion that happiness is a function of what happens in our lives? Are you kidding? Look around you, pay attention to the advertising messages we're bombarded with. Every product or service being promoted seems to base its appeal on the subtle—and sometimes not so subtle—promise that if we buy it, it will make us happy.

That conditioned desire for a Happily Ever After starts early—very early—in the first months of life. You'll recall that I am the father of three children whose ages span fifteen years. Over the course of those many years, I've read my share of stories to my children, beginning when they were too young—or so we thought—to really understand the words or concepts in those stories. Parents out there will quickly verify my observation that children are never too young to know if you try to skip a page or two.

Let's consider the stories we've read, over and over again, to our children. Those stories may have different characters and different plots, but they all end the same way: "And they lived happily ever after." Think about it. In the first few pages, our children fall in love with the characters. In the next few pages, what happens to those lovable characters?

They get into situations that are at least life-threatening, sometimes downright disgusting. Remember Hansel being caged by a witch who wanted to fatten him up and eat him? Can you imagine taking that story line to a publisher today and suggesting it as a children's book?

But back to the stories. So the characters get into difficulties too gruesome to imagine. Not to fear, however. In the final pages, not only do the heroes and heroines prevail over their tormentors, they live how? Why, "happily ever after," of course.

It seems to me that these stories, along with countless other conditioning influences, have effectively planted the Happily Ever After seed. At least partly as a result of their influence, we've embarked on a frantic, but futile, search for Happily Ever Afters.

This is such a prevalent phenomenon that I've created a model to illustrate the cycle in which we seem to be caught. I encourage you to refer to it as we work through some examples of how this cycle plays out in many adult situations.

The "Happily Ever After" Cycle

New and Exciting

One illustration of this Happily Ever After phenomenon is an experience that most of us have had. We've also had plenty of opportunities to observe others caught up in this experience. I'm talking about our very first day on the "best new job" we've ever had.

So tell me, how did you feel on that first day? I'm guessing it was a mixed bag, just like it was for me. On one hand, you were excited; for most people, that's probably the dominant feeling. But what other feelings did you have? Were you anxious, apprehensive—how about scared to death? Was there some of that, and if so, what was that all about?

No matter how happy we are about starting a new job, there is still a lot of uncertainty and, as a result, anxiety. "What if I don't live up to others' expectations?" might be one of the questions we deal with. So while there are some negative feelings, wouldn't you agree that the dominant feeling is some variation on excitement? The job is new and, by golly, we're excited!

How much of this excitement is based on our expectations of what the job will provide us? OK, probably a lot, and I'm not suggesting that it's unreasonable to expect opportunities such as new jobs to pan out. But too many people seem to show up with the belief that this job is their Happily Ever After.

Since we're adults, we probably won't be so bold as to share our expectations with others. You'll probably never hear a new employee say, "I'm so excited to be here because this is a 'happily ever after' for me." A word of advice here: If you do hear someone say that, I encourage you to find whoever hired that person and suggest that doing so was perhaps a mistake.

So we won't hear such declarations, but don't we see some evidence on that first day that indicates the new employee is excited? Let me ask that differently. What are some of the things we might see people do on their first day that we may never see them do again? See if these don't ring a bell. First-day people will generally show up early, wearing their very best "credibility costumes." They'll smile often, ask questions, and actually listen to responses. Chances are, they'll seldom look at clocks or their watches, they may work through lunch, and occasionally they've been known to stay late. These people are fired up! Now, how long does that initial euphoria last?

Well, it varies from person to person and situation to situation, but I think we can agree on a range. This initial excitement, and the behavior characteristic of that state, will probably last somewhere between forty-five minutes and six weeks. Does that sound
about right to you? And after forty-five minutes to six weeks, what happens to the "new"? Well, the "new" wears off, doesn't it?

The New Wears Off

If you're thinking back to your own first day on a new job, or to your observations of others on their first days, you can probably identify with the idea of the "new" wearing off. Hasn't that been your experience in so many situations? We get into something that's new, and our expectations are so high that we are plenty excited. And inevitably, over time, the "new" begins to wear off. We start seeing and hearing things we didn't see or hear during our first forty-five minutes to six weeks. Our perception of the situation begins to change, and seldom for the better. And as the "new" wears off, what happens to that initial excitement? It begins to wane.

Denial

As these changes occur, we often resort to the time-honored response: denial. We've all heard others say that someone they know is "in denial" about something. It's not difficult to spot people engaged in this behavior. They're the ones saying clever things like, "This can't be happening," "They can't do that," or "Surely they don't expect me to work with him/her."

Have you ever caught yourself thinking or saying such things? Do you think you might have thought or said such things forty-five minutes to six weeks after starting a new job? After all, you showed up expecting that job to be a Happily Ever After experience. When you started to pick up clues that it might not be that, the "rational" thing to do was pretend that what you were seeing, hearing, and experiencing "just couldn't be happening." Make sense? No, but when did making sense become a prerequisite for denial?

Unfortunately or fortunately, denial just doesn't work. No matter how hard we pretend that what's happening isn't, the evidence begins to mount, and we must conclude that this might not be a Happily Ever After job. Upon reaching that conclusion, we go to the next step in the cycle, and that's fear. What are we afraid of? Failure. Once again, we failed to find our Happily Ever After.

Fear, Anger, and Blame

Contrary to our best efforts at denial, we're afraid that "This really is happening," "I guess they can do that," or "Apparently they really do expect me to work with him/her." Oh, those icy stabs of fear, the realization that all the things we'd expected from this job may not be forthcoming. Tell me, is fear comfortable for you? No? I doubt that any of us are comfortable with fear, so we move—as quickly as possible—beyond fear and on to the next step in the cycle, anger.

Most of us are infinitely more comfortable with anger than with fear. Anger lets us focus on somebody or something "out there" to blame for an unhappy turn of events. Remember, we're convinced that the source of our happiness—or in this case, our unhappiness—is "out there," so all we need in order to let ourselves off the hook for our unhappiness is to find the "guilty parties." No problem.

In our new-job example, who are some of the people who might be blamed when things start to go wrong? Well, there's always the boss. If the person in charge had told you all there was to know about this job, you probably wouldn't have taken it in the first place, right? It's the boss's fault.

Then there are those malingering coworkers. If they'd carry their share of the load, things would sure be better. Of course, there are also the customers, patients, students—all those people and groups we must please. Then there are your competitors, out there lying about you, and your vendors, always gouging you. Can't forget the government and the politicians, whose sole objective is to make it more difficult to earn a living in this country. The list goes on and on, but there is one party who is conspicuously absent. Did you notice who that was? Of course, that would be the person doing the suffering, you.

Let's pause in our tour through the Happily Ever After cycle and consider these last two steps: anger and blame.

> It occurs to me that, in our country,
> we are so caught up
> in this outside-in perspective on quality of life
> that we set ourselves up for disappointment.
> As a result, we are becoming a society
> of professional victims.

When the quality of our lives isn't good enough, we're quick to blame the people and situations that we perceive as having let us down. We hold them responsible for the negative feelings we experience. It shouldn't come as a surprise that we blame those outside factors for our unhappiness, since we began this whole process by expecting them to make us happy. Victimhood is all the rage.

Just Give Up

Back to our new-job experience. Anger and blame lead inevitably to what I call "just give up," the next step in the Happily Ever After cycle. Now don't misunderstand me. When I say "just give up," I'm not referring to resignation. This step is more like a rehearsal for retirement. The people who get to this step still show up most days, but what can we count on them doing on the days when they're there? They'll probably do just enough to get by. Do you think there's much of that going on in the workplace today, people just going through the motions, not "making waves" or doing anything to "rock the boat"?

I'm convinced that there is a lot of "just give up" happening today, and I'm further convinced that many people spend most of their working lives in this step. Unhappy? You bet they are, but remember, since they've concluded that other people and situations are responsible for their unhappiness, they see themselves as helpless, and their situations hopeless. Does it sound to you like they've given up? It does to me.

Looking

Some of these professional victims stay stuck in this state of suspended animation, the Just Give Up step; but others take the next step. They go "looking." What are they looking for? Happily Ever After in the form of another job.

People in this step, the lookers, may find that the newspaper opens automatically to the classified ads every morning. Then one morning, they see it advertised: the "perfect job." Quickly they get on the phone and make two phone calls. Their first phone call is to their current boss, and when they get the current boss on the phone, what do they do? They can't quit the old job before finding something else, so they'll go into some sort of coughing, sneezing, gasping, wheezing spell symptomatic of a terminal disease, and then finally get enough breath to ask for a day of sick leave. Bosses, being somewhat rational people, will grant their requests.

After hanging up, the looker will place a call to the company advertising the position and make an appointment for an interview. Occasionally these "sick day" interviews pay off, and the looker is offered—and accepts—a new and exciting, Happily Ever After job. Now it's time to go back and see the old boss. This time the looker will thank the old boss for the opportunity to work there, explain that the work just isn't what was expected, inform the old boss that another position has been obtained, and give notice.

And two weeks later, how does our friend, the looker, feel the first day on this new job? Well, there's the anxiety associated with some uncertainty, but again, the dominant feeling is excitement, because this must be "it." Surely this job will prove to be that ever-elusive Happily Ever After. The cycle starts over again.

Chasing a Mirage

Let's go back to that last step, Looking. Where are these people looking? "Out there." And what are they looking for? Happily Ever Afters. Here's a conclusion I've drawn from the cycle, and from this last step: they're looking in the wrong place for something that isn't there.

I'm not suggesting that there's no such thing as a job in which we can be happy. What I am suggesting—actually, what I'm stating as a fact—is that there's no such thing as a job that will make us happy, and certainly not "ever after." There's a huge difference between the two.

> **Happiness on the job is certainly a possibility, but this quality of work life is not so much a function of chance as it is a function of choice.**

More on that distinction later.

Another Happily Ever After

I said we would look at a couple of situations that I believe illustrate the cycle, and the new job is one. Is there another area of life in America where you think this cycle might apply?

When I ask that question of audiences, there's one answer that I always get. That's right, always. The other area of life where people see clear evidence of the Happily Ever After myth is relationships; more specifically, marriage.

The marriage application of the cycle begins at the Looking step. If I were a single man, I would probably be looking. Being footloose and fancy-free, I'd be on the prowl, looking. What would I be looking for? (Let's keep it clean here.) The answer, of course, is Happily Ever After. I'd be looking for Happily Ever After in the form of Ms. Right. And when I meet her, I fall in looooove. OK, maybe it could more accurately be described as lust, but whatever we call it, it certainly qualifies as a euphoric state. Bells ring, birds sing, and my feet don't touch the ground, because I'm in love. I'm quite sure it will last forever, right?

Stop right here and think about this experience. How many of you have fallen in love? Probably all of you. How many of you have fallen in love this week? Never mind. Regardless of when or how often we have this experience, there are three common characteristics. First, we're euphoric; second, we see our new "love" as the cause of our euphoria; and third, we're convinced it'll last forever. Never mind the fact that we were just in—and out—of love with someone else last week.

Here We Go Again

And that brings up the question, How long does that euphoria last? As with the new job, this initial period of excitement will vary from person to person, but I feel sure the range is about the same—forty-five minutes to six weeks. It's cold, but true. The "new" wears off and the cycle plays itself out. The first stop is denial, where we might say or hear things like, "Man, I can't believe she said that." Next comes fear: "I'm afraid I've hooked up with another one just like that last one," followed by anger and blame. Who will we hold responsible for this unhappy turn of events? Of course, the first person is our partner, the person with whom we "fell in loooove," followed perhaps by that person's mother, the person who introduced us, and on, and on, and on. . .

As with the workplace example, anger and blame in marriage lead almost inevitably to Just Give Up, and I don't necessarily mean separation or divorce. You'll recall that when we were examining the new job, we said that the people who get to Just Give Up still show up, but even when they're there, they can't be relied on to do much. Same with marriage. The parties may continue to live together, but for all intents and purposes, one or both have simply given up. Sadly, there are probably many, many couples who spend years together physically, but without having any real substance to their relationships.

Among those in this Just Give Up stage, do you think there's much looking going on? Do you think there are many married people who are looking, outside the bounds of their marriages, for other people—-other people to make them happy?

Breaking the Cycle

That last step in the cycle, Looking, holds the key to breaking the cycle. In the first situation we addressed, first day on the new job, the cycle began when the lookers showed up to work, confident that they had found what they were looking for. And what were they looking for? A Happily Ever After job. When it became evident that those jobs were not going to live up to their expectations, the lookers transformed themselves into victims, and that's where many of them stay—on the job, but just helplessly going through the motions. Some of them became lookers again, searching for that ever-elusive, Happily Ever After alternative to the jobs that have begun "making them unhappy."

It's the same with our second example, marriage: looking for a Happily Ever After companion, finding someone who seldom lives up to those expectations, transformation into victimhood and, in some instances, a return to looking. In this situation, the lookers search for people to "make them happy" and replace those who are currently "making them unhappy."

Does all this sound nuts to you? Never mind the fact that most of us—and I am most certainly including myself—persist in some variation of this frantic search.

> **We continue to look in the wrong place
> for something that isn't there.
> We're looking "out there,"
> to the changing world of people and situations,
> for something and/or somebody to "make us happy."**

Is happiness, even prolonged happiness, a possibility? Of course, but it is not something that just happens to us. Nor is it something we can force to happen. It is, however, something we can choose, and that's both comforting and confusing.

A Case Study

Before looking at an alternative to the Happily Ever After cycle, let's look at a recent example of how the cycle played out in one specific industry.

The "new and exciting" condition that served as a starting point in this situation was the prolonged decline in interest rates, and the title insurance industry was one of the beneficiaries. One of the services title companies offer is closing real estate transactions, e.g., the purchase and sale of homes and other real property. Closers are the people who compile the mountain of documents that the parties must sign and/or initial at the closing table.

Closing services are also used by people who are refinancing their homes, so the low interest rates triggered a wave of refinance business. Business was coming to them, revenues were growing, and life was good. Talk about your "new and exciting." It wasn't too good to be true, but it was—like most other economic and marketplace conditions—temporary.

The pool of homeowners who were able and willing to refinance their home loans began to dry up, and interest rates began to rise. The "new" was wearing off, and as it did, many title company leaders recognized that as marketplace conditions were changing, so were the requirements for their companies' success. During the boom, closers were able to rely on "getting bought," but as the boom played out, selling was once again required.

So how did the closers react to all of this? Many of them recognized the need to be more proactive in their business development efforts. But many others didn't. Instead, they made classic Happily Ever After choices, starting with denial. They weren't so much denying that the refinance boom was over as they were denying the need to do anything different. They seemed to believe that if they just kept on doing what they had done throughout the boom—their closings—business would keep coming in, from somewhere.

As the evidence of change mounted, along with calls for them to become more engaged in business development, denial changed to fear. And for many of the closers, there were plenty of reasons to be afraid. Much of their business was going away. They were unsure about how, or if, that business could be replaced. They were also afraid of having to actually sell. As we all know, fear is not a comfortable feeling.

The fear was soon replaced by anger. Anger allowed them to focus on and blame all the outside factors responsible for the circumstance they found themselves in, the circumstances they found so frightening. While the objects of their blame varied, some of the most popular targets were the salespeople. After all, they were the people responsible for keeping the business pipelines full. Some closers blamed their managers, who were calling on them to help the salespeople sell their closing services to members of the real estate community. Here's a rhetorical question that was heard more than once: "Why do I have to do my job and also help the salespeople do theirs?"

Some of the closers just gave up. No, they didn't actually quit their jobs, although some of them threatened to do so if their managers insisted on their participating in the selling process. The Just Give Up stage can take many forms, and in this example, most of them were variations of passive resistance. Some closers were always "too busy" to meet with customers or prospects. Others reminded managers and salespeople that they were not salespeople and that selling was not part of their job descriptions. Grudging compliance does not often translate into effective business development behavior.

Finally, their trip around the Happily Ever After cycle reached the final step, or stage, Looking. They were looking "out there" to other people and/or for another boom to rescue them from the circumstances in which they'd found themselves.

> **People in this stage have already opted to look "out there" for the factors responsible for their suffering. Where else would they look for relief?**

Before leaving this example, let me again say that not all the closers took this path. Many of them, at the first indications that the "new" was wearing off from the boom, began to collaborate with their salespeople and managers to develop plans for procuring business from other sources. Leaders in the title companies with whom I've worked have labored long and hard to facilitate a smooth transition from the lender-driven market of the boom to the realtor-driven market that is re-emerging. As a result of their sustained efforts, more and more closers are becoming more engaged in the business development process.

This example illustrates two points that I'll cover in more detail later. First, there is a compelling alternative to the frantic, but futile search for Happily Ever Afters. And second, there are things that people in leadership positions can do to expand participation in that alternative process, which I refer to as the Relentless Search for Better Ways.

Choosing Happiness

While it's great to think that happiness is something we can choose, it raises a couple of questions. First, if I can choose happiness, does that mean I can also choose to be unhappy? Yep. Second, if that's the case, why have I been unhappy? Why in the world would anyone choose unhappiness?

Believe me, those are questions I've asked myself frequently, during and after my bouts with various forms of unhappiness, e.g., anger, frustration, resentment, or disappointment. Trust me, the list could be longer—much longer.

While I don't claim to have all the answers to those questions, I have drawn some conclusions from many of my life experiences, conclusions about the role I play in creating the quality of my life and about the contributions all of us can make to organizational success.

Victimhood vs. Accountability

Using the Happily Ever After cycle as a starting place—the status quo, so to speak—I've identified four requirements breaking that cycle and for achieving individual and organizational success. Those requirements, which I'll address in the following chapters of this book, are:

- Individual accountability.
- Change-friendly cultures.
- Broad participation in the Search for Better Ways.
- Leaders who are able—and willing—to lead.

In order for an organization to succeed, its individuals must bring about that success. As the people and situations that they encounter change, those individuals must change the ways they do things. They will often find it necessary to perform different tasks.

Encountering and having to make such changes creates fertile ground for the victimhood behavior that is characteristic of the Happily Ever After cycle. So the first, and possibly the most important requirement for organizational success is to root out tendencies toward victimhood and replace them with a characteristic that is highly touted, and is written and spoken about with great enthusiasm, but is seldom practiced:

> **INDIVIDUAL ACCOUNTABILITY**
> **The First Requirement for Winning**

CHAPTER 2 SUMMARY
THE "HAPPILY EVER AFTER" CYCLE

- Most people seem to have concluded that their happiness or unhappiness is an effect, the result of something that takes place in their lives.

- Their happiness with new and exciting experiences is usually short-lived. The new inevitably wears off, and so do the initial excitement and happiness.

- Fearing that they've once again failed in their frantic search for a "Happily Ever After" experience, e.g., new job or relationship, they hold the experience responsible for causing their unhappiness.

- Believing that they are at the mercy of factors beyond their control, they do the very thing guaranteed to prolong their unhappiness; they just give up.

- Some people continue searching for different experiences, ones that will make them happy, but most of them continue looking in the wrong place for something that isn't there.

- As they continue in this frantic search, the experiences will change, but the people having those experiences will not. The cycle plays out again, and again, and again…

- Happiness and unhappiness are not so much functions of chance as they are functions of choice.

- In the following chapters we will look at the requirements for making better choices.

Chapter 3

From Victimhood to Accountability

As I write this chapter, it is election season. Does it seem to you that it's always election season? This is the *real* season, however, a presidential election year. The airwaves are filled with declarations of just how wonderful things will become if one or the other of the candidates is elected. Talk about your Happily Ever After promises.

Not surprisingly, one of the pledges being made is for "accountability": accountability in government, accountability in the Oval Office, and on, and on. To hear the candidates talk, one might think we're on the brink of a new era of individual accountability among elected officials. That's until you reflect on past elections, preceded by campaigns with the very same sort of pledges. As I said in the last chapter, accountability is highly touted, and is spoken and written about with great enthusiasm, but we just don't see much of it in action.

Here's a working definition I've come up with:

> **ACCOUNTABILITY**
> Acknowledged Ownership of the Choices We Make,
> And the Consequences of Those Choices

The operative word here is "acknowledged," as in recognizing and claiming my ownership not only of the choices I make, but also of the *consequences* of those choices. That's where it starts to get difficult, right?

I mean, come on, who could quarrel with the fact that if it's a choice I made, I own it? It's mine. Nobody else made that choice, so nobody else can own it. Could others have influenced me and the choice I made? You bet, but when you get right down to it, they didn't make the choice. I did. It may be an ugly or silly little choice, but it's all mine. I own it, for better or worse.

It's also obvious that for most choices there will be consequences. When I make a choice that yields consequences, regardless of whether those consequences are good, bad, or in between, I own them. I am responsible for them; I am accountable. No ifs, ands, or maybes. Accountability—for everyone other than politicians, apparently—is acknowledged ownership of choices and their consequences.

Change Requires Accountability

For example, the decision to provide skills training for people in an organization is not one to be taken lightly. Training can be quite expensive, both in terms of the organization's investment in the trainers and their materials, and in the time participants spend away from their work. The only reason an organization makes such an investment is in the belief (suspicion or hope?) that there will be significant returns on the investment. The most sought-after returns are performance improvements on the part of those who attend the training. Make sense so far? So where does accountability come in?

Participants will make critical choices about how they use the training, and the consequences of their choices become the returns, or lack of returns, on the training investments their organizations have made. Unless participants show up with open minds and are willing to consider alternative ways of performing tasks, or even alternative tasks, they will probably get little from the training, and their organizations will get little in the form of returns.

But there's more. Those participants must also be willing to *act* on what they have learned, to actually try new things back at the workplace.

> **Willingness to consider alternatives is a choice, and so is the willingness to try those alternatives.**

Too often participants in such training show up expecting or demanding a Happily Ever After trainer or materials. They insist that they "be changed" by the training, expecting that somehow, there will be an automatic transformation in how they perform back on the job. Ain't gonna happen.

There are certainly differences in the quality of trainers, training materials, and techniques being taught, and OK, I'll even go so far as to concede that some training is absolutely useless. But when there is some merit in the techniques being taught and some competence on the part of the trainer, participants' choices become the critical factors. The participants are ultimately accountable for the effectiveness of the training.

OK, that was fairly easy, especially since we're speaking in very generic, almost academic terms. Most people can live with that definition of accountability. Now, let's take it to the next level: the choices we make and some of their likely consequences.

Thoughts and Feelings are Choices

The choices most of us think of are physical or behavioral, the things we choose to do or say and how we do or say them. Those are certainly important choices, and many of their consequences are readily apparent. For example, the words you choose, and the tone of voice you use, will produce consequences in the form of people's reactions. It's fairly easy to acknowledge our physical choices. And the ways of improving them are also relatively easy to identify, if sometimes difficult to implement.

There is another category of choices, however, that is much more subtle, but with consequences that are far more powerful than those of their physical "cousins." *Mental* choices, our thoughts, are ones that often escape scrutiny since they are usually automatic. I mean, how many of your thoughts occur without your being consciously aware of them? Who knows, but let's agree on a "scientific" measurement: a whole lot of them.

Back to my earlier comment about quality of life. You'll recall that I suggested that feelings are the standards we use to assess the quality of our lives. Good feelings translate into good days, and vice versa. I also described, in Chapter 2, the critical roles we play in creating the quality of our lives, in spite of our conviction that it's the people and situations "out there" that have all the power. (See the Happily Ever After cycle.)

This is where we must start making a dramatic break with "tradition" and begin challenging some of our basic assumptions about cause and effect. Do the people and situations we encounter, the outside factors in our lives, have some impacts on us? Of course they do.

> **People and situations do have influence over us, but ultimately, it's the choices we make about outside factors that really matter.**

Those choices are instrumental in creating our feelings, and our feelings impact our behavior. Finally, our behavior determines our effectiveness in dealing with those people and situations.

Individual accountability is all about choice and consequences, and I think this would be a good time to look at some examples of real-world situations in which we make powerful choices and the options from which we choose when making them.

Dealing with Setbacks

The Relentless Search for Better Ways is the process of acknowledging or anticipating the changing requirements for our success and adapting to meet those requirements. This ongoing search will pay off, but rarely without some setbacks.

> **When individuals and organizations embark on such a process, they must do so secure in the knowledge that setbacks are not only possible or probable, they are *inevitable*.**

Hasn't that been your experience in life? Anytime you set out to make worthwhile changes in just about any area, even if you've worked to anticipate problems and have developed contingency plans, what always happens? Like the rest of us, you encounter unexpected problems, or setbacks.

Setbacks provide us with valuable, but difficult, opportunities to acknowledge and improve the choices we make. I am convinced that, without even being aware that we're doing so, we always—that's *always*—make choices about how we respond to setbacks. The two options available to us are victimhood and accountability. Which option do you think is more popular in our culture?

Most people will readily concede that victimhood is the hands-down winner. Why? Because it's so darn easy to be a victim. You're off the hook, it's somebody else's fault, and so it's obviously up to them to do something about it. Looking back to the Happily Ever After cycle, we can see the sequence of steps in the victimhood response to setbacks: fear, anger, blame, and finally, "just give up."

Let's take a closer look at these two options, Victimhood and Accountability, and let's keep it lighthearted. After all, most of us are expert victims, so the last thing we need to do is compound our victimhood by beating ourselves up. Since it's the more popular of the two, let's start with victimhood.

Victimhood

It's not exactly an official word, but it sure has a nice ring to it, doesn't it? Sounds like a word a person could get comfortable with; that's as it should be, since it's a condition with which most of us seem to be mighty comfortable. But maybe it's not so much that we're comfortable, since some variations on victimhood are anything but comfortable. Maybe it's an easy way out. Regardless of where you stand on the issue of comfort, you're probably no stranger to victimhood.

After carefully scrutinizing many of my life experiences and my antics as the experiences were playing out, I've identified what I believe are two important aspects of victimhood.

1. Mistaken beliefs about the power of outside events—the foundation of victimhood.

2. Unwillingness to acknowledge that we can control our responses to these events, the choice that relegates us to the status of victims.

Both represent choices we make as we grapple with the people, situations, circumstances, and events that comprise our life experiences. We'll begin with the foundation.

Victimhood and Beliefs

Victimhood, in all its variations, is based on a widely held, but mistaken belief. Before I reveal the belief that I see as the culprit in this whole victimhood thing, let's spend a minute or two on beliefs in general. I'm sure we all agree that they are mighty powerful, right? So what are they? They are the "truths we hold to be self-evident." They are the explanations we've accepted for what is true and not true, for why people and things behave the way they do. They are strongly held opinions, our convictions about the "way things are."

Those are our *real* (internal) beliefs, but not necessarily our *professed* (stated) beliefs. Surely you recognize the difference. Consider an historical example about the "self-evident truths," famously documented by our founding fathers. Remember? Things like, "all men are created equal." We need go no further to recognize the gap between professed and actual beliefs. For a hundred years after the declaration of that "truth," slavery existed in America. And for another hundred or so years after slavery was abolished, racial segregation stood in direct opposition to that "truth," the professed belief on which our country was founded.

Back to beliefs, the ones we internally hold to be true. Would you agree that they exert powerful influence on our lives, specifically on many of the choices we make? Would you also agree that it's possible that some of our beliefs may be mistaken? OK, not yours, but isn't it possible that others' beliefs may be a bit off-target? Finally, aren't mistaken beliefs just as powerful as the ones that are valid?

> **The fact that they are mistaken, invalid, inaccurate, or just plain wrong in no way diminishes the power of beliefs.**

You want an example? You've got it.

Think back with me to the years prior to 1492. I know, you were very young, but think back and tell me, what was the prevailing belief about the shape of the planet? Flat as a fritter, right? Was it actually flat? Unless there's been a pretty dramatic rounding since then, the answer is no, it was not flat. So we can conclude that even though it was widely held, the "earth is flat" belief was mistaken. Mistaken, maybe, but it still exerted a pretty powerful, limiting influence over the people who held it. The limitation? No long boat trips!

Challenging Mistaken Beliefs

As I see it, victimhood has at its core a mistaken belief, and that mistaken belief exerts powerful, limiting influences over all of us who hold onto some variation of it. The belief goes like this: "What happens 'out there' determines how I feel." Think about that for just a minute. "What happens out there," meaning the people, situations, circumstances, and events we encounter, all the changing phenomena we must contend with, "determines how I feel." This belief is at the heart of victimhood, because it encourages us to abdicate any role we play in determining the ultimate quality of our lives. It not only makes such abdication OK, it tacitly discourages any alternative belief or perspective.

OK, some of you are having a tough time with this one. You're pretty sure you don't harbor any such nutty belief; so let me do a little research here, a short "experiment." I want you to think before answering this question. Ready? Now, can you think of people in your life who upset you? Well, hey, that didn't require much effort, did it? I came up with a couple dozen real quick. So what we have here is an example of this mistaken, outside-in belief at work. These peoples' behavior is something that happens "out there" and upsets us (determines how we feel). Somehow these people have assumed sufficient control to actually determine our feelings. Is that scary? Happily, there's a solution.

What I want you to do is make a list of all these people who upset you. If that will take entirely too long, limit the list to your top fifty, the ones who really get to you. After you finish your list, I want you to go immediately to your phone book, to the Yellow Pages, and turn to the section for mental health professionals, psychiatrists or psychologists. Next, I want you to select one of these good professionals and make appointments for all the people who upset you. Surely you understand my logic. When all those people "get fixed," you'll be OK.

No, don't really do all that. Just content yourself with the knowledge that your aversion to other peoples' behavior is not unique to you; the rest of us are in the same boat. My point here is that "the boat" we're in is this mistaken belief that the people and situations in our lives are responsible for how we feel, for the quality of our lives. Now that's one leaky boat.

> Our outside-in, mistaken belief about
> how the people, situations, circumstances,
> and events in our lives create or cause our feelings
> is the foundation, the basis for our victimhood.

We use that belief to victimize ourselves by establishing unenforceable "rules" for our happiness. We begin with the belief that what happens "out there" determines how we feel. Since we all know that we would like to feel happy, or some version of happy, we act on our belief by establishing guidelines for what must, or must not, happen "out there" in order for us to be happy. They're really not guidelines, they're more like addictions, the things we're attached to getting or having, and the things we're averse to. Some people might call them "pet peeves." You got any of those? Yeah? Me, too. Let me share a couple of my personal favorites to illustrate what I'm talking about.

Vigilante Victimhood

Shopping for groceries is something I occasionally do. When I do go to the grocery store, it's to pick up just a few items, so I almost always qualify for the express line. I know some of you are already nodding your heads and creating some mild forms of psychotic rage.

> There have been many instances when,
> in the middle of a crowded grocery store,
> I have transformed myself into
> "The Express Line Police"!

Is an explanation necessary? The allowable number is ten—that's *ten*! If you can't count to ten, you have no business in "my" express line. Here's how this malady plays itself out. I roll my cart up, containing an allowable number of items, to the end of the express line (there are always people ahead of me). When I stop my cart, I don't know what it is, but something takes over my body. I move off to the side of my cart and begin doing inventory, counting the items in the other peoples' carts. Don't be snickering and shaking your head. I'm guessing you've done the same. I almost always catch a "perp," someone who has violated the store's "ten-item rule," one that I heartily support. Now it could be that the "perp" hasn't violated the letter of this rule, but may instead have violated *my* version. Here's what I mean. Let's say you have three tomatoes. If they're in a bag, I'll let them slide as a single item, but if they're not in a bag, they count as three items, and you'd better not try sneaking them through as a single.

After detecting violations of these "rules", I notice a serious deterioration in the quality of my day. I experience unhappy feelings such as anger, resentment, and frustration. And who do I blame for these feelings? Here comes another list. I certainly blame the "perp," but trust me, the list of guilty parties does not end there. I'll spread the blame to include the checkers, who could and should do a better job of policing their lines. I might even blame the store owners for not installing closed-circuit cameras and hiring burly bouncers to evict the "perps." By now you're starting to realize that I'm no stranger to victimhood, and who better to write about it than a seasoned veteran?

This entire scenario provides a great example of how I use the mistaken belief that what happens "out there" determines how I feel to victimize myself.

> **I victimize myself by establishing and insisting that others adhere to my "rules" for what must happen in order for me to be happy.**

I know that my express line antics are the result of choices I've made, and I know that other people have made different choices. I know all that because occasionally my wife, to whom I've previously referred as St. Barb, and I will shop together, and on some of those occasions we qualify for the express line. And here's the part you'll find difficult to believe: I've never seen Barbara count the items in another person's cart. I don't know what's the matter with her. Not only does she never count those items, she finds it mildly disturbing when I do. And she's right. I succeed in victimizing myself, and I perpetrate that behavior by blaming my victimization on others. Lord, is there any hope for me?

More Vigilante Victimhood

You like that example of addictions at work? Here's another one of mine that might resonate with you folks who don't obsess over items in grocery carts. I have some hard-and-fast "rules" about how others must operate their motor vehicles when sharing the roadway with me. This is an area where there is absolutely no room for compromise, since the physical well-being of other drivers, passengers—maybe civilization as we know it—is at stake. Or at least that's the way I approach it.

One of my "rules" involves the distance other drivers must leave between the front of their vehicles and the rear of mine. I'm referring, of course, to the scourge of happy motoring, those vile, subhuman tailgaters. Do I detect a roar of approval from you, dear readers?

Actually, my experience with tailgaters has proven quite helpful in identifying and evaluating the steps by which I victimize myself. Here's the way I've broken it down. First there are my perceptions, what I see. Next, there are my thoughts about what I'm seeing, thoughts that are based on my beliefs and perspective. My thoughts are followed quickly, almost instantaneously, by my feelings. The time lapse between thoughts and feelings is so short that it is undetectable. Since we're left with the feelings, we often overlook the thoughts that precede them. Finally, there's my behavior.

The sequence looks like this:

- Perceptions (what I see).
- Thoughts (how I process what I see).
- Feelings (my emotional state; the quality of my life at the moment).
- Behavior (the things I do or say, and how I do or say them).

The last one seems to get the most attention.

So, I'm driving along when, in my rearview mirror, I see an approaching tailgater rapidly closing the distance between his or her car and mine, clearly intent on violating my roadway "rule." At once, I begin formulating thoughts about the tailgater. In the interest of propriety, I won't elaborate. Suffice it to say that my thoughts are not all that charitable, and they're so automatic that I probably don't even consciously acknowledge them. That's where my problems begin to multiply. What I do notice are my feelings, and they're usually some variation on a common theme: anger. Since I pay no attention to my thoughts, but wallow in my feelings, it's safe to conclude that I have succeeded in once again abdicating any responsibility for creating my feelings by transferring ownership of the choices that created them to what's happening out there—specifically, to the tailgater.

Now we get to the "nutso" part, my behavior. Keep in mind that what triggered this whole episode was another driver getting "too close" to my vehicle. What do you think one of my strategies has been? Why, of course, to do the very thing guaranteed to get that other vehicle closer to mine: I slow down. And all the while, I glare at the other driver in my rearview mirror and ask rhetorical questions such as, "How do you like driving five miles an hour?" It goes downhill from there.

Let me pause here in this sad commentary on my experiences as a driver, and call your attention to the phrase I used when referring to these addictive thoughts. I've called them unenforceable "rules". They are clearly "rules", since they represent the parameters of what we've decided is acceptable behavior, but they are also *unenforceable*. Think about your pet peeves or addictions. I'm willing to bet that many, maybe even most of them relate to what happens "out there," to outside factors over which you have absolutely no control, and probably precious little influence. For example, how many tailgaters pull up alongside you and ask permission before gating your tail? How many express-line crashers consult with you prior to unloading their carts?

> **We've abdicated our happiness
> to people and situations
> over which we have no control,
> and if ever there was a recipe for "unhappiness
> squared,"** *that's it.*

Being Right or Being Happy — a Choice

Let's go back into the tailgater scenario and look more closely at the four steps we use to victimize ourselves and consider some alternatives, some ways we might be able to reduce our suffering and our bizarre behavior.

Why do people tailgate? OK, there could be thousands of reasons, but the one overriding explanation is they want to drive faster than we are driving. Fair enough? So the question remains, "Why?" We'll probably never know. Since we don't know their motives, we're left with assumptions. Do we generally assume the best motives or the worst? I'm guessing we'll err on the side of worst, and therein lie both the cause of, and the solution to, our problem with tailgaters.

What if you knew that, lying in the lap of the tailgater, was a sick or injured child and that the driver's only motive for wanting to drive faster than you was to get that child to a doctor? Let's consider the impact of such knowledge on the four steps we previously used to victimize ourselves.

Our perception will probably be the same. We'll see another vehicle approaching us from the rear, moving at a speed that is closing the gap between us. Our thoughts will change rather dramatically. Before we knew about the injured child, what were our thoughts? Basically, we were probably thinking of what the other driver must do in order for us to remain happy: slow down and maintain the "correct" distance between our vehicles. But knowing about the child, we'll probably be thinking only about what we can do to help that driver get to the hospital or doctor. Do you see the difference here? It's not a small or even subtle shift, it's 180 degrees. Our feelings will also swing rather dramatically. Before knowing about the child, we probably experienced some form of anger. But, knowing about the child, we'll have compassion, empathy, and sympathy for the other driver. Again, a pretty significant shift, wouldn't you say?

Finally, how will we behave? Instead of our anger-induced, obstructionist behavior, we'll make every effort to get out of the other driver's way. And after they've passed us, we'll probably send that driver and passenger on their way with a sincere hope—maybe even a prayer—that they will arrive safely at their destination.

Yes, you say, if there really were a sick or injured child in that car, we would be perfectly willing to opt out of victimhood. What does that tell you? That you have the power to do so, and if that's the case, what possible reason would you have for choosing to remain a victim? Oh, of course, I almost forgot, unless there really is a sick child, you and I insist on others following our "rules". Naturally, we'll bend those "rules", but only if there is basis in fact for our doing so. Bottom line, and you've heard this before:

> **Most of us would rather be right than happy, even when being right just doesn't matter.**

Try this. The next time you look in your rearview mirror and see a tailgating incident beginning to unfold, simply say to yourself, out loud, "sick child." A word of caution is in order here. Don't say it out loud if there are other people in your vehicle. It can cause funny looks.

Just saying or thinking "sick child" will remind you that you are in the process of making choices that will impact the quality of your life for the next few minutes, maybe even the next few hours. It might remind you that the other driver's motives are unknown and probably unknowable to you, so you're left with assumptions. So why not assume something that would justify relaxing your otherwise just and reasonable "rules" for how others must operate their motor vehicles? Will there really be a sick child? Probably not, so you'll be wrong. But guess what else you might be? Happy, or at least happier. OK, so maybe just less unhappy, but in any case, it's progress.

Victim Choices

Victimhood, as a state, is a consequence of two questionable choices we've made. The first is our decision to accept the mistaken belief or belief system that what happens out there determines how we feel. The second is how we use that belief to establish unenforceable "rules" for what must/must not happen out there in order for us to be happy. Now let's look at some choices we make when we encounter the inevitable conflicts between our "rules" and what *does* happen—in the real world.

We've already agreed that such conflicts, or setbacks, are inevitable. These setbacks can be serious. However, it is the choices we make *about* the setbacks that are often more powerful and have more impact on our lives than the setbacks themselves.

> **Too often, we compound the negative impacts of setbacks by making victim choices about them.**

For example, denial certainly qualifies as a victim choice. Just pretend that the setback didn't happen. Ignore it, and maybe it'll go away or correct itself. Sound familiar? Blame, wallow, and quit, three of the steps in the Happily Ever After cycle, are other examples of victim choices. No, I'm not dismissing the possibility that other people may, and often do, contribute to the setbacks we experience, nor am I suggesting that we ignore the roles they've played. What I am saying is that if our response to setbacks is limited to identifying the "guilty parties," our chances of recovering or learning from those setbacks is remote at best. But it sure is easy, isn't it?

"Wallowing" is a word that conjures up some interesting visual images, but let's limit our discussion to the emotional wallowing that characterizes victimhood. What are some of the feelings in which victims are prone to wallow? Self-pity comes to mind, and so do others, like anger, frustration, resentment, suspicion, distrust, disappointment, and on it goes. Wallowing is also an easy alternative to actually trying to do something about setbacks. In fact, helplessness is probably another good wallow.

Quitting, or "just give up," is the ultimate victim choice. Deciding that their situations are hopeless, that they are helpless, and not even considering the possibility that they could learn something from a setback, victims inevitably quit. No, they don't always leave the jobs or the relationships or whatever situations they're blaming for their unhappiness. But for all intents and purposes, they've quit.

Waiting, wishing, and hoping are also victim choices. Even people who have essentially quit may still wish and hope for "salvation" or "rescue" from their unhappiness. They're too devastated to do anything themselves, but they're still waiting for things to change or for somebody else to make things get better. They're wishing things were better and hoping that someday, somehow, they'll get better.

When they encounter life's inevitable setbacks, victims *do* make some choices. They deny, blame, wallow, throw in the towel, and content themselves with waiting, wishing, and hoping for somebody to change those outside factors that are making them so miserable. They are, indeed, victims, but not so much victims of the setbacks as they are victimized by the *choices* they've made about the setbacks.

Actual vs. Contrived Victimhood

Before we leave victimhood for that more lofty alternative, accountability, let's concede that there are setbacks that are so severe, that have such powerful negative impacts on us, that we can say with great confidence that we were legitimate victims. Thank God, you're thinking, there are circumstances in which it's OK to be a victim. Without "blessing" it as OK, I will agree we can, indeed, be victimized.

Have you ever been robbed, mugged, swindled, or cheated? We can be victimized, and in the wake of such setbacks, most of us will probably make some of the victim choices I've just described: denial, blame, wallow, wait, wish, hope. I'm guessing that in life's most severe examples of victimhood, most of us do not quit. And that's a key difference between legitimate and contrived victimhood. In the former, we suffer, struggle to come to acceptance of the setback or loss and finally, we recover. In contrived victimhood, there is a tendency to blow setbacks out of proportion and/or to actually pour energy into sustaining the negative feelings we associate with those setbacks.

For example, have you ever been angry, maybe legitimately angry, with another person? If you answered no to that question, please put this book down and begin writing one of your own. Of course, most of us have been angry with other people. Have you ever remained angry with another person long after the event you used to trigger your anger in the first place? Another way of asking this question is, have you ever held a grudge against another person? At what point in this process did you have to remind yourself of the event and put some energy into conjuring up that old anger?

Time for another personal example. I spent a tour of duty in Vietnam, and while I was there, an American celebrity made a public appearance in Hanoi. For those of you too young to remember, Hanoi was the capitol of North Vietnam, and the North Vietnamese were the folks with whom our allies, the South Vietnamese, were having a little tussle. The only way an American could get to North Vietnam was under cover of darkness, as in sneaking across the demilitarized zone that separated north from south, become a prisoner of war or, as in the case of this American visitor, be willing to speak out against the American war effort. The person was Jane Fonda, and she most definitely was there to speak out against what we were doing.

When I heard about this, I assumed a victim role and was angry at what Ms. Fonda had done. I was convinced that my anger was justified, that she had indeed provided comfort to our enemies, and in doing so, might have encouraged them to continue fighting. OK, they would probably have continued fighting whether or not Jane Fonda visited them, so her actions probably did nothing to prolong the conflict. As a Marine officer I was angry, but here's the real story. I held onto my anger at the lady for years. Long after we had left, long after the restoration of diplomatic exchanges between our country and the now-united Vietnam, I insisted on remaining angry at Jane Fonda. (I'm sure she was absolutely devastated by my grudge.)

Many of you might say that I was justified in holding onto that anger, but who suffered? Was it Jane Fonda? Of course not, it was me. I was not just a victim, I had become a "professional victim."

Here I am, traveling around the country speaking and writing about accountability, about acknowledged ownership of the choices we make and the consequences of those choices, all the while holding a lady I've never met accountable for my anger. What a hypocrite! I had been busily victimizing myself and blaming her. I wasn't just a victim; I had become a living example of "professional victimhood."

As I see it, there are legitimate victims and there are "professional victims." Legitimate victims are any of us who suffer as a result of choices others make and/or because of circumstances beyond our control. "Professional victims" are those people who, in response to life's inevitable setbacks, always play the victim card. They look "out there" for the causes of, and relief from, their suffering, their victimhood. I'll sum it up this way:

> You can't be "drafted" into victimhood.
> All of us "professional victims" are volunteers!

Achieving Accountability

So far we've explored the dark world of victimhood. Hopefully, we've shed some light on how we create it and some of our antics while under its spell. By way of review, I've offered up what I refer to as an outside-in belief system: "what happens out there determines how I feel" as the basis for our victimhood. What I'm saying is that, with such a belief, we quite naturally look "out there" for the sources or causes of our feelings. When we're unhappy, we seldom consider the possibility that we've played any significant role in creating our unpleasant feelings. We may be unhappy, but by golly, we're off the hook. Armed with that belief system, we've established unenforceable "rules," our demands and expectations for what must/must not happen out there in order for us to be happy. Since the people and situations out there don't always conform to our "rules" (how's that for understatement?), we're often unhappy.

As an alternative to that quagmire, I offer accountability, which I've defined as acknowledged ownership of the choices we make and the consequences of those choices. Accountability, like victimhood, has its basis in an underlying belief system.

Over the past several years, I have developed and regularly refined my core values. Let me quickly say that they have not yet reached the status of actual beliefs; I'm not claiming to always practice them. They are my professed beliefs, and through effort, including plenty of times when I've fallen far short of the mark, I'm incorporating them into my life. They are progressively becoming the basis for—and more strongly influencing—the choices I make.

One of my most important core values reflects the belief system I see as the foundation of accountability. It is an inside-out belief, and it goes like this:

> **I am solely accountable
> for the quality of my life.**

Many people see this as a rather extreme position, and when compared to the attitudes of our "victim culture," it is extreme. Let me clear up a couple of possible misinterpretations, and then we'll see if it seems less extreme.

When I say "solely accountable for the quality of our lives," I don't mean that we are somehow responsible for the people, situations, circumstances, events, or any of the other factors we encounter "out there." In fact, we have only limited influence over those factors.

You'll also remember my saying that while those outside factors can impact us negatively, the choices we make *about* those factors are often more powerful—have more impact on our lives—than the factors themselves. Since I'm the only one who can decide what those factors mean to me, I am solely accountable for making those choices. And since those choices, more than the factors themselves, will determine the quality of my days, I am solely accountable for the kind of days I'm having.

Contrast this belief with the one I've identified as the basis for victimhood, "What happens out there determines how I feel."

The distinction—inside-out versus outside-in—is obvious, and these two beliefs will support different perspectives.

A New Point of View

Perspective. Now there's an interesting word. As it is often used, perspective is the way we look at things. Here's a variation on that definition:

> **PERPSPECTIVE**
> The Place From Which We Look At & Process
> The Outside Factors In Our Lives.

If we look at the same scene from different places, our perceptions of that scene will vary. Seems to me that our belief systems become the places from which we look at, and assign meanings to, what we see.

Try this example: What does it mean to be fifty? I'm sure you'll agree that it pretty much depends on where you're looking at fifty from. Turning fifty means something different to a person looking at it from twenty-five than it does to another person looking at it from seventy-five. To the younger person it probably means "old," with plenty of negative connotations. To the older observer it might mean "young," or certainly "younger," and probably has more positive characteristics. It's the same number, used in the same way and viewed at the same time, in the same context by two people with two different perspectives. Those two people will see and interpret it differently, based on their different perspectives, the places from which they look at, and assign meanings to, being fifty.

When "professional victims" look "out there," they're looking for the sources or causes of their happiness or unhappiness. When the outside factors in their lives conform to their demands and expectations, they're happy. When their "rules" are violated, these "professional victims" probably won't deal very effectively with the people and situations they've encountered. Caught up in their victimhood, they may point fingers and wail about their plights, but they probably won't engage in any constructive effort to deal with the setbacks and improve the quality of their lives.

Accountable people also look "out there," but while they acknowledge deviations from what they have hoped for or expected to happen, they won't waste a lot of their time and energy railing against "the injustice of it all." Instead of the denying, blaming, wallowing, waiting, wishing, and hoping that characterize their more victim-like colleagues, they'll make more accountable choices and almost always deal more effectively with setbacks.

> **The basis for accountability is a commitment to the proposition that we are all *solely accountable* for the quality of our lives. One technique I've found effective for actually practicing such an inside-out alternative to victimhood is acknowledging and improving the choices I make when I encounter setbacks.**

Making Better Choices

Our victim conditioning has led us to establish "rules" for what must/must not happen out there in order for us to remain happy. When we encounter events that violate some of our "rules", we have excellent opportunities to reflect on how we've used those "rules" to victimize ourselves. In those instances, we have an accountable alternative to wallowing: we can put some effort into upgrading our "rules"—our addictions—to *preferences*.

Look, I'm not suggesting apathy as a workable alternative to victimhood. The outside factors in our lives most certainly impact us, sometimes unpleasantly. In the real world, setbacks are inevitable. I don't know about you, but I don't want anybody on my team who doesn't care—is apathetic—about setbacks.

> **Remember, the choices we make about setbacks are often more powerful than the setbacks themselves.**

More specifically, our behavior in response to setbacks will either compound—or, preferably, mitigate—the negative impacts those setbacks have on us and on our organizations. And I'm sure you'll agree that our mental/emotional states dramatically influence our behavior.

Before we can expect to engage in constructive behavior, we'll probably have to free ourselves from mental and emotional wallowing, and that requires us to do something about those pesky "rules". The "rules" I'm referring to are the ones we've established and then cling to when choosing the quality of our days.

If you think back on your childhood, you can probably recall some of your adult family members' favorite platitudes or admonitions, the wisdom they attempted to pass along to you. If your experiences were anything like mine, you probably also recall wondering how people so obviously demented could possibly have been related to you. In short, many of the things those adult people said, credible or not, went in one ear and out the other.

Having pretty well mastered victimhood at an early age, I would occasionally engage in bouts of whining. I found teachers particularly troublesome, and I was not bashful about reporting their indiscretions to my parents. Whining in the presence of my father almost always elicited one of his standard responses: "Boy (I was sixteen before the man learned my name), get over it and get on with it." Don't you love it? Without having to waste any of his valuable time listening to all the details, Dad just cut right to the chase, and in the finest tradition of fathers everywhere, he provided his pat solution to my perceived problem.

> "Get over it
> and get on with it."

Reflecting back on that advice, I've been struck by its wisdom, and I have discovered how it can become the basis for upgrading our "rules"—addictions to what must/must not happen out there—to preferences. I'm not sure I ever heard my father use the word "accountability," and I would be surprised if he'd ever read any sort of self-help literature. I'm real sure, however, that in spite of my years of thinking, reading, writing, and speaking about this alternative to victimhood, I'm still well below the level of accountability he demonstrated in his life. I'm also sure that when we encounter life's setbacks, Dad's simple suggestion can become a model for acknowledging and improving the choices we make.

You'll notice that "getting over it" precedes "getting on with it," and that makes sense. Before we can respond effectively to setbacks we'll need to get past, or work through, our initial mental and emotional reactions. Many of those initial reactions are classic examples of victimhood.

Get Over It!

A first step in getting over it is acknowledging the setback. When we encounter something that's unpleasant, that impacts us negatively, instead of denying it or ignoring it and hoping it goes away, let's acknowledge it for what it is, a setback.

As you might suspect, setbacks come in many different forms. For our purposes, let's agree that any deviation from our "rules"—and that would be any event, situation or behavior that doesn't conform to what we've decided must or must not happen in order for us to be happy—is a setback. Given that broad definition, can there be any doubt that setbacks are not just possible or even probable? They're inevitable. We'll be given plenty of opportunities to work on upgrading our "rules" to preferences, and we begin that process by acknowledging them.

Here's a tip for acknowledging setbacks. Catch yourself experiencing victim feelings like anger, frustration or resentment, and after consciously acknowledging those feelings, identify the event, situation or behavior that you used to *create* those feelings. That's the setback, the deviation from your little "rule."

The second step in getting over it is to do some appropriate and rational "grieving". Remember, I'm not endorsing apathy. When we encounter setbacks, I would expect there to be some less than happy mental and emotional responses, some "grieving." But pay particular attention to the adjectives I've used to describe those responses: appropriate and rational.

> **Our grieving should be appropriate, or proportional, to the setback.**

A classic victim choice is to react to all setbacks as if they were life-threatening. Have you ever blown an event or experience out of proportion? We all have. After acknowledging such an event by catching ourselves doing some form of "grieving" that is disproportional to the event itself, we have an opportunity to consider the probable impact the setback will have on us, and then limit our grieving to what is appropriate.

Annie to the Rescue

Occasionally we'll need help in recognizing that our "grieving" is disproportional to the event we viewed as a setback. I have someone in my life who is more than willing to provide such help. That person is my daughter, Annie.

Annie is one of those people who just seems to breeze through life. She is first and foremost a social person. She loves people, and people love her. She is irrepressibly happy; she loves to have a good time, and she's mighty good at finding plenty of healthy opportunities to do so.

In addition to her busy social life, Annie is a volleyball player. Every year for the past 5 years Annie has played on her school teams from August through November and then on club teams from December through the following May or June. That adds up to a lot of games, matches and tournaments, and not all of them have turned out the way we'd hoped. As you would expect, Annie's teams have lost some of the games and matches they've played, and afterward the girls have expressed their disappointment and "grief" by crying a few tears and occasionally assuming more than their share of the responsibility for the losses. Those setbacks have provided great opportunities to compare the girls' appropriate, rational "grieving" with a less functional variety.

You're probably thinking that, as her dad, my "grieving" over the losses would reflect my understanding that it's volleyball, not life or death, right? If you'd ever seen me "in action" at Annie's volleyball tournaments you'd know better. Without going on and on about my antics during the games, let's cut to the aftermath of ones we've lost.

After congratulating members of the other team, our girls meet with their coaches for a short post-game discussion. The coaches review the game, pointing out the good and not-so-good aspects of the girls' play and offering suggestions for improving the latter.

After these post-game sessions, the girls rejoin us parents who are eager to offer our thoughts. Some parents limit their feedback to words of support and encouragement. But I have been known to follow a higher calling, sharing with Annie my observations about the game, the play of all participants (on both teams), the coaching and the officiating. In order to ensure that she gets the full benefit of my post-game analysis, I've occasionally dealt with losses as if the fate of the world was at stake. OK, I'll concede that the feelings I've exhibited have been disproportional to the gravity of the setbacks.

And how does Annie respond? After looking at me as if I were some form of alien being, she'll inform me that she and her teammates are going for pizza and that she needs money. The game is over, they lost and now she's ready to move on.

It occurs to me that in spite of my good intentions, my expressions of "grief" about their losses have occasionally been inappropriate and irrational. But hey, I'm trainable. When my post-game ranting has been disproportional to the loss, Annie has stepped up as my teacher. By her behavior she has demonstrated what appropriate, rational "grieving" looks like. And then she's taken my money and gone for pizza, leaving me to plan my strategy for the next game.

Beyond "Grieving"

Recovering and learning from setbacks require us to do more than just grieve. Our grieving must not become a substitute for dealing with the setback. We'll need to go to the second step, "getting on with it." Disappointment about a setback can become an incentive to recover or learn something from that setback. Disappointment is a feeling that we can resolve by taking action. Devastation, a popular choice for victims, becomes a reason for not acting. How could anyone expect devastated people to do anything about what devastated them?

Our "grieving" over setbacks should also be rational in terms of its intensity and duration. Intensity, as you know, is often evidenced by behavior. For example, I can be frustrated about bungling a three-iron shot and still be semi-pleasant company for my golfing partners. Or, I can go into a rage about the errant shot and heave my three-iron into a wooded ravine. My frustration about the bad shot may be appropriate and even rational, but rage, as evidenced by my hurling the offending club, is neither appropriate nor rational. (Note: This is a purely hypothetical example, as someone who writes and speaks about accountability would never engage in such questionable behavior.)

Duration is another criterion for defining rational "grieving". Have you ever had a "bad" day that you attributed to an event that occurred, say, on the way to work? OK, have you ever had a bad day turn into a bad week, month, or longer? At what point do we choose, on some level of consciousness, to pour energy into prolonging our grieving? My prolonged anger toward Jane Fonda was an example of irrational grieving. That, coupled with my three-iron launches, should serve as a reminder that anyone as familiar as I am with victimhood is surely qualified to write and speak about it—with more than a little credibility.

Are There Limits to Accountability?

A question I'm often asked when speaking on the topic of accountability is, "Aren't there limits to our potential for accountability? Surely there are some circumstances or events in which victimhood is the only option available." I can't claim to know the answer to that question, but based on my experiences, I'm convinced that our potential for accountability, like our potential for most things, is far greater than what we've demonstrated. Let me share another experience I've had that illustrates that potential.

My Dad — My Accountability Coach

I grew up in Abilene, Texas, in a wonderful family setting. As with so many people of their generation, my parents seemed to assume different, but equally important, roles in our home. My father, like his father before him, was the breadwinner, the "head of the household." Does that mean he lorded it over our mother? Hardly. She was the homemaker, the loving and nurturing parent, but she was not at all reluctant to assume the role of disciplinarian on those frequent occasions when my sister misbehaved and on those, oh so rare, occasions when I did. Two events that occurred after my sister and I were grown precipitated a shift in our parents' roles. They were also harbingers of later, more dramatic events that called forth amazing examples of accountability.

The events were two near-fatal heart attacks suffered by our father. After the second one, we were told that he needed bypass surgery. Naturally, we were all at the hospital on the day of the surgery and were later delighted to hear that the operation had been successful. Dad was then placed in intensive care. Every hour for just five minutes, we could each take turns visiting him. Before the first visit, I recall my mother passing along some rather firm instructions. She reminded us that Dad had "always been there for us." and she proclaimed that, "By George" (my mom's form of profanity), "we're going to be there for him." She went on to suggest that if we couldn't be positive and supportive, if we couldn't set aside our own fears and concentrate on boosting his morale, we should just stay out. My sister and I each promptly assumed the position of attention, rendered a hand salute, and followed her instructions.

Understand that this take-charge potential had always been alive and well in Mom, and she decided that, under these circumstances, it was the card she should play. And did she ever play it! Over the course of Dad's recovery, she took charge. When he needed to be nurtured and supported, she was there. When he needed his backside kicked—figuratively, I think—she was there to administer the boot. As you would expect, Dad went through many months of physical and emotional challenges, but he made a complete recovery. I have absolutely no doubt that Mom contributed mightily to that recovery, and her willingness to step up to the plate and assume something of a new role serves as one example of accountability.

Was Mom dealing with some setbacks? How about Dad's two near-fatal heart attacks? Did those setbacks have negative impacts on Mom? Definitely. Was victimhood an option? As always, it was most certainly an option, and given the roles Mom had played throughout her marriage, she could probably have played the victim card by claiming unfamiliarity with taking charge. But what did she do? My friends, my mother "got over it and got on with it."

Never denying the gravity of the situation, Mom was the first to acknowledge the life-threatening nature of the events and the potentially negative outcome of the surgery, given the damage to Dad's heart. She looked the event, my father, my sister, and me in the eye and acknowledged that what we were dealing with was a significant setback.

And she grieved, but her grieving was both appropriate and rational. She realized that she would have to be a source of strength for all of us, and she was. Does that mean she was apathetic? Of course not. She probably worked through all the steps in the grieving process, but she did so in ways that were appropriate (proportional, not so much to the gravity of the situation, but to the impact her grieving would have on others), and rational. She endured months of uncertainty, mini-setbacks and scares, but her strength and her faith carried us all.

Finally, she got on with it. She quickly realized what she must do, and she did it. She became our "rock," and she single-handedly facilitated Dad's recovery. I guess you're starting to make out the headlines: This event, along with all the other characteristics she exhibited in her life, made this little woman from East Texas not just my mom, but a true heroine.

> If I ever need examples of what
> accountability under adversity looks like,
> all I have to do is recall my mom's heroics
> during Dad's recovery,
> and my dad's behavior when Mom died.

The Next Chapter

It was late afternoon, several years after Dad's brush with death that he called me and said that Mom had just suffered a massive heart attack. It didn't look good. We loaded up and sped to Abilene, and I was blessed to be with her when, several days later, Mom passed away without ever regaining consciousness. A huge setback, wouldn't you say?

Naturally, we all grieved, but the person my sister and I were most concerned about was Dad. He and Mom were married for forty-four years, and too often, when a companion of that duration passes, the surviving partner soon follows. We were so very concerned about how Dad would respond to Mom's passing, and during the months following her funeral we were in very close contact with him. We've always been close, and during this time of grieving, we became even closer. We visited often, and my dad and I spoke on the telephone every Sunday evening. That's where his indomitable spirit, his penchant for accountability became evident to me.

It was about ten months after Mom's death, a Sunday evening, and Dad and I were having our weekly chat. Actually, "chat" is probably not the correct word; my dad was anything but "chatty." Many of you probably have family members or friends with whom you have regular phone conversations, right? Have you ever noticed that one of you is the "call terminator," the one who usually closes the proceedings? That was my dad. Not given to a lot of small talk, when he decided we'd said all that needed saying, he'd say something like, "Well, it's been good talking to you, Jimbo, and I'll talk to you next week." Click, buzzzzz—he was gone.

I knew something was up on this Sunday evening when, after we'd completed what he generally considered enough conversation, he paused. My dad hardly ever made nonverbal pauses, so when he paused this time, I paused with him. After a few seconds (sure seemed longer to me), he made the following announcement, "I've got a date."

My friends, I didn't get many opportunities to toy with my dad, so I seized this one. I'd heard what he said, but I pretended to need a repeat, so I said, "You've got what?" Having to repeat himself was not something Dad was accustomed to, so, with just a hint of irritation in his voice, he said, "I said, I've got a date." So, as soon as we could, our family loaded up and headed for Abilene. We couldn't wait to meet the new lady in Dad's life.

Viola's husband had passed away a year before Mom, and they had all gone to the same church, so they knew each other and knew of each other's losses. It seems that the date Dad was referring to was not their first. There had been something of a courtship in progress for a few weeks before he felt it necessary to inform me. I was absolutely delighted, and after meeting this wonderful lady, we were all even happier.

So there I was, playing a new role in the life of my father. Up to that point, when there was someone new, a "candidate" for membership in our family, I was the one bringing that person to meet the family. But here I was, "the family" to whom the lady was being introduced. We all went out to dinner together, and after dinner, we returned to Dad's house for coffee and further conversation.

Have you ever noticed how conversation—when it seems to be called for—becomes more and more strained and difficult? Luckily for the other family members present, they had, in me, a professional speaker. Rising to the occasion, I would save everyone from those dreaded silences by uttering profound things like, "Man, wasn't that steak great?" or the one that seemed to push them all to the breaking point, "Lord, I am full!" After a few renditions of this cleverness, Dad announced that he and his wonderful, beautiful lady were going to be married.

> **Our potential for making accountable choices is pretty much unlimited.**

The two principal characters in this situation had both experienced significant setbacks, losses with potentially devastating impacts. But that potential devastation required their cooperation, and they were having none of that. They could have chosen to give up, to relegate themselves to the role of victims, and we all know the likely consequence of such a choice. But they made a different choice. They chose to continue living their lives actively, to enter a relationship that would allow them to give and receive the love and support that had characterized their entire adult lives. They chose to acknowledge their ownership of the choices they made—how they responded to the passing of their former spouses—and the consequences of those choices, their impact on the quality of their remaining years.

If you compare the magnitude of their losses with other, far less traumatic setbacks, you can see that the choices they made stand in stark contrast to the choices we often make after those relatively insignificant deviations from our "rules." They grieved, and then they got on with their lives.

Actually, the story gets better. After they got married, Dad and Viola decided to sell their respective houses and build a new home together. It seemed appropriately symbolic of the new life they were beginning together. My Dad decided he would be the general contractor on the project, which was somewhat surprising since he'd never built anything in his life. When I asked him why he was taking on such a task, he said he was quite confident that only he would do the quality work he expected. Knowing his attention to detail—the minutest of detail—I could only mutter a silent "amen" to this first reason. He went on to say that he was also thinking about starting his own homebuilding company.

The home was completed, and the newlyweds spent almost two years of happiness in it together. It was like Dad had been totally rejuvenated; he spent those years happier than I'd seen him in a long time. And he went out pretty much the way he would have wanted. On the last day of his physical life, Dad got up early and played eighteen holes of golf with his best friends. He came back to his still-new home, showered, got dressed, and fell dead. It was quick, and apparently painless.

As I said earlier, my Dad probably never used the word "accountability," but in his life he demonstrated just what it means.

He grew up on a farm in East Texas, endured the Depression, went off to World War II, participated in the liberation of the Dachau concentration camp, married his childhood sweetheart, and with her made a life for us that was far, far better than anything either of them had ever had. Like so many of his generation, he didn't make a lot of noise, but he made a big difference in so many people's lives. When he was dealt "bad hands," he didn't spend a lot of time blaming, wallowing, waiting, wishing, or hoping, and he certainly never quit.

Guess you can see that he was a man of his word. The words he shared with me have become the basis for my perspective on accountability. And those words? "Get over it and get on with it." The "boy" part is optional.

CHAPTER 3 SUMMARY

- Accountability is acknowledged ownership of the choices we make and the consequences of those choices.

- The people, situations and circumstances we encounter have impacts on us, but ultimately it's the choices we make about those factors that really matter.

- In the Relentless Search for Better Ways, setbacks are inevitable.

- We always make choices about the setbacks we encounter and how we'll respond to them.

- The 2 options available to us are victimhood and accountability.

- The choices we make about setbacks are more powerful (have more impact on us) than the setbacks themselves.

- Victimhood begins with the underlying belief that what happens out there determines how we feel.

- Based on that mistaken belief, victims establish unenforceable "rules" for what must and must not happen out there in order for them to be happy.

- Victim choices about setbacks include: blaming, wallowing, quitting, waiting, wishing and hoping.

- All "professional victims" are volunteers.

- Accountability begins with the underlying belief that we are solely accountable for the quality of our days.

- Based on that belief, accountable people reduce or even eliminate their emotional attachments to what happens out there. They still care, but they refuse to base their emotional states on factors over which they have no control.

- "Get over it and get on with it" are the choices accountable people make about the setbacks they encounter.

CHAPTER 4

Change-Friendly Cultures

Several years ago—OK, more than several—I learned to fly, and today I am the holder of a license to fly single-engine airplanes. I haven't actually flown an airplane in many years. But the way the regulations work, if I could pass a physical and perform basic flying maneuvers satisfactorily for an instructor pilot, I could once again rent and fly airplanes. Rest easy, I'll not be doing so.

During my pilot training, I was exposed to a new "language," terms and phrases that relate to aircraft performance and pilot proficiencies. One phrase that has stuck with me, and one that relates well to the need for "change-friendly" organizational cultures, is "behind the power curve." Here's a brief description of that concept.

For pilots, power is the force required for forward movement through the air. Let's just refer to that as flying. Since the airplane is always being pulled downward by gravity, some degree of power is required to maintain altitude and sustain flight, preventing the heavier-than-air machine from falling to the ground, an event to be avoided. If the pilot reduces power, the airplane will descend.

To arrest the descent and level off, power must be added. Getting "behind the power curve" means that the rate of descent is too great, and/or the distance between the descending airplane and the ground is too small, to allow for a leveling off—no matter how much power is added. Before the added power can stop the descent, the airplane will strike the ground. Striking the ground in an uncontrolled fashion is what we highly trained pilots refer to as crashing. (I hope you'll excuse my use of so many technical terms.)

When an airplane is descending, some degree of power must be added just to stop the descent and level off. If the pilot wants to climb back up to the original altitude, the one at which the descent began, even more power must be added. The power required for either a correction or a return to the plane's previous status (altitude) exceeds what would have been required had the aircraft not begun its descent. This situation is known as being "behind the power curve."

Now that you all feel qualified to engage in "pilot speak," let me use that aeronautical example to illustrate a key point:

> **Creating and sustaining change-friendly cultures is a requirement for breaking out of the Happily Ever After cycle and achieving individual and organizational success.**

Organizational Culture

The words "environment" and "culture," which I'll use interchangeably, have gotten a lot of attention lately. The phrases that seem to be most common are "corporate culture" and "work environment." A reasonable place to begin is by getting a handle on just what these terms mean.

For most organizations, especially businesses, associations, practices, and other commercial enterprises, there is a gap—often a rather wide gap—between their professed and *actual* cultures or environments. One of the phenomena we've seen over the past decade or so is a profusion of organizational mission statements being declared. They are often typeset, printed, framed, and displayed prominently in these organizations' facilities, often in locations accessible to customers, clients, or patients. I'm not suggesting that all such documents are misleading, but my experience with many organizations has caused me to question their commitment to their mission statements, which they would probably hold up as a reflection of their cultures.

Can you think of an organization in which the behavior of people in leadership positions seemed to conflict with that company's professed values? Can you say "Enron"?

Here are some lines from Enron's "Statement of Values" in its 2000 annual report:

> "We treat others as we would like to be treated ourselves."
>
> "We do not tolerate abusive or disrespectful treatment."
>
> "We work with customers and prospects openly, honestly and sincerely."

Really? In light of everything that has happened since this report was issued, how did these words play out in the real world? Can we honestly conclude that the decisions made by people in leadership positions at Enron reflected those professed values?

I wonder if "others" in that first sentence was meant to exclude the thousands of Enron employees who were unceremoniously shown the door after years of loyal service. I guess that executives lying to employees about the value of employee-held company stock, while dumping their own, wouldn't qualify as "abusive or disrespectful treatment." It would be interesting to hear the testimony of Enron's former customers about how the company worked with them "openly, honestly and sincerely."

My point here is really quite evident. Words are fine, but the proof is in the actions taken. You can profess to have any sort of culture you'd like, but labeling it doesn't make it so. Just ask some of Enron's former employees and customers.

At the risk of offending those who insist on creating complex, multifaceted models for everything, I see organizational culture or environment as being most clearly reflected in behavior. For example, I can get a pretty good idea of an organization's actual culture or environment by observing how decisions are made and implemented. The way decisions are made and implemented will reflect some of the more fundamental components of an organization's culture or environment.

> **Regardless of how many documents, badges, banners, and marketing pieces are used to convey a sense of organizational culture, the proof is in the behavior.**

Principles, values, and commitment to process improvement certainly are important elements in organizational cultures, and those underlying, foundational factors will play out in behavior. For example, a culture that includes staff members in decision making—and I'm not talking about an exercise in democracy—

certainly speaks to an organization's principles, values, and commitment to process improvement. The principle holds that people in the organization are capable of—and accountable for—more than just performing the tasks listed on their job descriptions. The value in play here is the potential value of all staff members' input. The commitment to process improvement is evidenced by the Relentless Search for Better Ways.

The scope, magnitude, and speed of change in today's world have pretty much eliminated complacency as an effective organizational strategy. Yesterday's products, services, delivery, strategies, and practices may already be obsolete. Viability in the real world requires organizations to engage in a Relentless Search for Better Ways, and participation in that search must extend beyond the upper echelons of management. In spite of the emphasis on broad participation in decision making, as evidenced by the elevation of "empowerment" to buzzword status, too many organizations still rely exclusively on a relatively small group of people to create plans and agendas. For most organizations, that small group does not include many, if any, of the people whose efforts will be required to effectively *implement* those plans.

OK, I'm getting a bit ahead of myself. I'll speak to the issue of expanded participation in Chapter 5. But before we can realistically expect the people who heretofore have been excluded to participate actively in the Relentless Search for Better Ways, we must create and sustain cultures that will support their participation. And just what sort of culture would we be looking to create? Does "change-friendly" ring a bell?

The Willingness to Consider and Try

So what, exactly, is a change-friendly culture? Well, it is a combination of highly complex, cosmic components, which I've used to create an esoteric model. Did your eyes just glaze over?

Relax. "Complex," "cosmic," and "esoteric" are alien concepts to me.

> **Change-friendly cultures are ones in which there is widespread willingness to consider and try alternatives to the status quo.**

The status quo includes many components, some of which are not open to debate or subject to change. For example, most people are unwilling to alter or modify their principles, so when embarking on the Relentless Search for Better Ways, let's begin by identifying the components that we'll view and treat as unchangeable.

As I see it, the status quo includes things like principles, values, purpose, strategies, practices, processes, policies, products, services, structure—and on and on. Most of those components are fair game when looking for better ways, but there are exceptions.

For example, I'm not willing to dramatically alter, or even slightly modify or compromise, my principles. I suspect that most people in your organization feel the same about theirs. So when we embark on our search for better ways, let's begin by identifying and defining, where necessary, the principles and other components that we view and treat as unchangeable. Getting a good handle on principles and values is mighty important, since we'll need to consider and use them when choosing alternatives to all the other components of our status quos. You may identify alternatives that appear attractive, but if they are not consistent or compatible with people's principles and values, they are not truly better ways. People simply will not engage in activities or practices that cause them to compromise their principles.

Willingness to consider and try alternatives is the key to creating and sustaining change-friendly cultures. Not surprisingly, this willingness must originate with people in positions of authority, people who can either select or "bless" alternatives. I'll speak more about the role of leadership in this process in Chapter 8. For now, let me say that a key driver in organizational cultures is leadership behavior. To those of you in such positions, whether in the workplace, home, school, church, or community, please pay particular attention to my emphasis on willingness to consider and try alternatives.

> **Facilitating the Relentless Search for Better Ways is one of your most important roles. Creating and sustaining Change-Friendly cultures are two key steps in that process.**

Change-friendly cultures are ones in which ideas are actively solicited and freely shared. Within this criterion, there are two distinct roles: asker/listener and sharer. Both are equally important. One of the challenges for managers who are sincerely trying to include staff members in the decision-making process is the reluctance of those staff members to participate.

In change-friendly cultures, questioning the status quo is not only allowed, it's *encouraged*. Someone must initiate this process by encouraging people to question, and when encouraged to do so, people with questions must step up and ask them.

Is Your Open Door Really Open?

Before you can realistically expect people to offer up their suggestions or to question the status quo, you must convince them that it's safe to do so; you must make it clear that there aren't many sacred cows in your organization by encouraging people to offer their suggestions for how to do things better. As you might suspect, leaders' responses to others' questions and suggestions will determine just how safe it is to continue offering them.

> **"Willingness to consider"
> means willingness to listen non-judgmentally.**

As people become more comfortable questioning and suggesting, the more proficient they will become at identifying areas in which better ways are needed. If there's any truth to the rumor that as the people and situations in our lives change, so do the requirements for our success, then acknowledging or anticipating those requirements will enable us to make the changes necessary to our success. We will be able to develop and implement more effective strategies and tactics for meeting our new requirements, and that's certainly an example of playing to win. Ignoring or disregarding the need to make changes is a recipe for getting our rear ends handed to us. That's Texan for "losing."

I'm convinced that the environments we create and sustain will strongly influence the choices made by the people working in those environments. Change-friendly cultures support accountability, as evidenced by the choices people make in response to the inevitable setbacks they will encounter. Making accountable choices is also essential for leaders seeking to sustain those change-friendly cultures. When there's a lot of experimenting and learning going on, there will be plenty of mistakes, and plenty of mistakes are a good indication that the environment is change-friendly. It's also an indication that the organization and its people are playing to win.

How You Choose to Play

Playing to win versus playing "not to lose" is another distinction that applies to individual and organizational success, and it's not just for athletes. Most of us can recall instances in which our favorite players or teams employed either one of these strategies, with mixed results. Fact is, there are plenty of circumstances in which playing "not to lose" is not only OK, it makes perfect sense.

For example, if I'm playing in a golf tournament, and on the last tee I find myself leading the field by five strokes (how's that for a harmless little fantasy?), I'll probably not be taking a lot of risks on that last hole. Instead of hitting high-risk shots—like trying to drive the ball over that wooded ravine into which I threw my three-iron in an earlier example—I'll probably hit a shorter, safer shot. Remember, I'm up by five shots. What's the payoff for taking the risk of losing my ball—and possibly another three-iron—if I try to get across the ravine in one shot? Even if everyone else manages to do so, they've still only made up one shot; I'm still leading by four. God, I love this example.

Let's look at some of the differences between these two approaches, knowing that the culture in which people work will strongly influence the way they choose to "play."

Playing Not to Lose

In the previous example, I explained that there was not sufficient value to justify the risk of hitting a more-difficult golf shot. There are circumstances in which taking such risks is not prudent, but there are other situations in which taking risks is *essential* to winning. If, instead of leading by five strokes, let's say I came to the last hole trailing by one or two strokes. What that means is I have this last opportunity to make up those strokes and win the tournament. The leader may opt for the safer shot, but if I'm to have any chance of winning, I must try for the more difficult one. I can still opt for playing it safe, hoping that the leader makes mistakes, but if I do, I greatly increase the likelihood that I will lose.

In organizational settings, this penchant for playing "not to lose" often manifests itself in an unwillingness to incur short-term risks. If there's any merit in looking for and trying different, and hopefully better ways, then there is justification for incurring the risks associated with that sort of experimentation. When we step out of the old, familiar ways and begin trying alternatives, we can expect to encounter discomfort, and even mediocrity, since we've gotten out of our "comfort zones." Fact is, we probably won't perform new or different versions of old tasks as well, initially, as we performed the old ones. Would you agree that those are short-term risks?

After some period of familiarization, we'll become more comfortable and, with practice, we'll become more proficient. And if these new ways do indeed allow us to increase our effectiveness, enhance our market viability, and achieve more of our objectives, then wouldn't you agree that the long-term payoffs justified the short-term risks? Unwillingness to incur risks, usually short-term risks, is a characteristic of playing "not to lose."

The more I've thought about it, the more convinced I've become that playing "not to lose" is almost *encouraged* in our society. Here's an old saying that expresses the essence of this approach: *if it ain't broke, don't fix it.*

Have you heard that one? Of course you have. Who hasn't? I'd guess you've even used it occasionally, because it seems to make sense, doesn't it? If something's working, just leave it alone. Don't create problems where none exist. Don't make waves. OK, there's a long list of similar sayings, so I'll leave it there. Let's take a closer look at this pithy old saw and see if we can't shoot some holes in the logic on which it's based.

"If it ain't broke, don't fix it" seems to imply that as long as there's no serious dysfunction, we should leave well enough alone. The implication is that until something breaks, until it becomes absolutely unworkable, there's really no reason to "tinker with it." But has that been your experience? Or, have you found that if you ignore something until it breaks, sometimes it is unfixable? Even if it can be brought back to a functioning state, the resources required to do so probably exceed those that would have been necessary to at least maintain it.

Let's go back to my highly technical aeronautical lesson in which I described what it means to be behind the power curve. If a pilot ignores the aircraft's altitude until it begins to erode, it will take even more power to arrest the descent and bring the aircraft back to its original altitude than it would have taken to maintain that altitude in the first place. However, if the rate of descent is too great relative to the aircraft's proximity to the ground, no amount of added power will prevent a crash. That same principle can be applied to organizational viability.

Given the scope, magnitude, and frequency of change in today's marketplace, waiting for something to "break," ignoring critical strategies, processes, and relationships until they become ineffective, can be the kiss of death. Hence my emphasis on engaging in a Relentless Search for Better Ways. "Playing to win" is another phrase that describes that search, and a change-friendly culture is essential to sustain it. Playing "not to lose" may be a choice, but it is absolutely not a viable strategy for organizations in competitive environments.

Playing "not to lose" may seem to be a safer alternative to playing to win, since there is avoidance of risk. But what we're avoiding in the short term will often jump up and smite us further down the road.

> The payoff for avoiding short-term risk
> may be temporary comfort, but the price
> of this short-term comfort might take the form
> of greater long-term risks.

Those long-term risks can be—and often are—more significant than their short-term cousins.

I've referred to accountability as acknowledged ownership of the choices we make and the consequences of those choices. Playing "not to lose" is most certainly a choice, and the likely consequence of that choice, *when made habitually*, is losing. Winning requires both offense and defense, and playing to win includes healthy emphasis on the big "O."

Playing to Win

Change-friendly cultures, ones characterized by a willingness to consider and try alternatives to the status quo, encourage playing to win. People in such environments understand that they incur risks when experimenting with alternative practices. After comparing the risks to the likelihood that the alternative practice will prove more effective and yield desirable payoffs, participants will decide whether or not to pursue that alternative. They understand that even if the alternative doesn't pay off, they will not be condemned for having given it a try. Sure, there will be some "post-attempt" evaluations, probably including some discussion of the process they used when selecting and implementing the alternative, but their initiative in trying the alternative will be applauded. Their efforts will be acknowledged for what they are, examples of playing to win.

Creating and sustaining change-friendly cultures requires initiative, commitment, and perseverance, much like beginning and sustaining long-term relationships. Marriage comes to mind. Creating a change-friendly culture is one thing; sustaining it presents us with a different set of challenges. In that regard, it's similar to the difference between "falling in love" and sustaining a long-term marriage.

Falling in love is a piece of cake, right? I'm sure we'll all agree that this is the easy part. Now, how about staying married to the same person for more than forty-five minutes to six weeks? While falling in love—beginning a relationship—is relatively easy, sustaining a healthy, loving, and mutually supportive long-term relationship is considerably more challenging, isn't it?

Think back to my earlier reference to how the people and situations in our lives change, creating new or different requirements for our success. That phenomenon applies to marriages, and it most certainly applies to work environments or cultures. Creating a change-friendly culture may not be as easy as falling in love, but it is probably going to be much easier than sustaining it.

Remember, setbacks are inevitable, especially in an environment characterized by experimentation (trying alternatives to the status quo).

> The way people respond to those setbacks,
> *especially the way people in leadership positions respond,*
> will determine whether the environment
> will remain change-friendly,
> or become just another failed experiment.

Lessons From the Home Front

Back to the home for a look at players and their roles in creating, sustaining, and functioning in change-friendly cultures. I've always found the home to be a great place for teaching and learning lessons that apply to every area of life. It seems to me that the most successful parents, the ones who prepare their children to function well in the real world, create and sustain change-friendly cultures in their homes. Here's an example from my experiences with our children.

Every one of them has pretty well mastered many life skills, and the skill I'm thinking of here is walking. Let's flash back to the day when our youngest, Jessie, first attempted this feat. Barbara and I were with her in the family room, when suddenly Jessie decided she'd had enough of creeping and crawling, and took her first step. Actually, she'd been standing by the coffee table, holding herself up by clutching its edge.

After carefully considering her options, weighing the risks of failure against the likelihood of success and the potential pay-offs—the ability to run from her parents—she concluded that the risks were justified, so she let go of the table. OK, if that's the thought process she used, she didn't share that with us. Remember, the ability to communicate verbally was still down the road. First walk, then run, and then develop the vocabulary necessary to explain why you tried to escape—or something like that.

Back to Jessie's first step. She let go of the table, put one foot in front of the other, shifted her weight, and promptly fell. Happily, Jessie was well-padded. She was wearing a disposable diaper, she had ample layers of baby fat, no discernible elbows or knees, and she really didn't have far to fall. There was no damage done. She had demonstrated her willingness to consider and *try* an alternative to the status quo. Her performance also illustrated what we can expect when such experimentation occurs—a setback.

We know that young children try new things. They are, by nature, experimenters, and during their first few years of life they learn plenty of important skills. Their learning is characterized by many setbacks, and that's where people in leadership positions—we parents—can facilitate and even expedite their learning by creating and sustaining environments in which they are comfortable with the process. Seems to me that such environments are change-friendly, and parents' responses to their children's failures will serve to encourage or discourage their efforts to learn.

Before I get to Barbara's and my enlightened responses to Jessie's attempt to walk, let's look at the relative difficulty of sustaining, as compared to creating, change-friendly cultures in our homes. Most parents will agree that our children's early experimentation with things like walking and talking are relatively easy to deal with. After all, these little experimenters are cute, and the consequences of their inevitable failures are not that bad.

After these early stages, our children's growth becomes more difficult, not so much for them as for us parents. After walking and running, we get to the bicycles and, in order to teach them and support their learning, we must often run—nay, sprint—alongside them as they weave and bump down driveways, roadways, and rocky trails. The part of this and subsequent phases that I've found most trying is not so much the physical support. I'm perfectly willing to install, remove, reinstall, re-remove training wheels. And to hold the bike upright while the child mounts and remounts.

The part I find troubling and challenging is how to provide the emotional support they're seeking. They want to try, but they don't. They want me to hold them up, but they want me to let go, and they're not too happy about my inability to figure out just what they do want. At the risk of alienating approximately half of you, I've found this characteristic to be particularly pronounced with my daughters.

So we've progressed from walking to bike riding, and you parents of young people at or past the age of sixteen know what's coming next. This is when it becomes mighty difficult to maintain that old change-friendly culture, right? For some unknown reason, the people who we rely on to make such decisions have determined that, upon reaching the age of sixteen, people may become licensed drivers. If ever there was reason to question authority, that's it. Speaking on behalf of parents everywhere, I am absolutely convinced that no one under twenty-one has any business behind the wheel of a motor vehicle. There, I've spoken.

When our children begin tackling the more challenging—and potentially dangerous—life skills, many of us parents begin to question the wisdom of sustaining change-friendly cultures. We agonize over their progress. We spend countless hours worrying about all the dire consequences of the mistakes they could make and the mistakes other drivers might make, mistakes that would put our children's lives in peril.

What's the point? Creating and sustaining change-friendly cultures is inherently risky. There *will* be mistakes, setbacks, and failures, and the consequences of those inevitable occurrences will be negative, and they will be felt.

> **Trying new things is risky,
> but it is a preferable alternative
> to clinging to the status quo.**

An Invitation to Experiment

In organizational settings—businesses, associations, firms, practices, campuses—there are similar phases or stages of experimentation. When we first invite people to experiment, to look for and try alternatives to the way they've done things, or even to try different things, their initial efforts will probably be somewhat tentative. People may be hesitant to experiment with what they see as major components of the status quo, especially when doing so might be perceived and treated as being politically incorrect. What that means is most people will not quickly do anything that might incur the wrath of the "powers that be."

If the people in positions of leadership, the folks who encouraged experimentation, respond supportively to early experimentation and the inevitable setbacks, the participants in that process will become bolder. While they may have held back in the early phases, they'll now be willing to tackle bigger icons, to incur greater risks. Like their early efforts, these newer endeavors will sometimes end in failure. These failures will have more impact on the organization, and the people who were supportive of early, safer experiments may now be inclined to "draw the line" and call off the search for better ways. While I agree that none of us should be given carte blanche to incur risks, I am absolutely convinced that trying to limit the search to alternatives you're comfortable with would be like telling your sixteen-year-old that she can't learn to drive because you're afraid of the consequences.

In the workplace, you can't have it both ways. If you're going to encourage people to experiment, if you provide them with reasonable parameters and the freedom to experiment within those parameters, you must be willing to accept setbacks. I'll tell you something else that's inevitable, and that's the impact of your responses to those setbacks on people's willingness to persevere in the search for better ways. You can invite them to take risks, but if by your behavior you condemn them when their experiments fail, you're asking them to incur a risk you're not willing to take.

The minute we believe that leaders disapprove of something we've done, we'll probably think twice before doing it again, even if those people seemed to have encouraged us to do it. If you tell me with your words that you want me to experiment, and reassure me with words of support when I encounter setbacks, I'm probably going to give this experimentation thing a try. But if, with your behavior (your responses to my failures), you send me a disapproving message, if I interpret your behavior as disapproval of what I've done (experiment) and even of me as a person, you can be sure that for me, the environment is anything but change-friendly. You can also be sure that my future participation in the Relentless Search for Better Ways will be half-hearted, at best.

In the home, our children drag us, kicking and screaming, into new realities. After all, they do grow up; they will try new things and they will make mistakes. But by resisting the inevitable, we forfeit any meaningful opportunities to assist the learning and growth that would mitigate the risks. The better alternative is to stay the course, to sustain the change-friendly culture we've created. We created these environments when our children were small, as were the risks. By persevering, and sustaining those environments, we can support, facilitate, and expedite our children's growth through even the most-challenging phases. Having said all that, I'm still convinced that twenty-one is plenty young for a driver's license. Ha!

So how did Barbara and I respond to Jessie's failed first attempt to walk? As you would expect, we wrote the child a bad efficiency report, docked her a day's pay and sent her to her little room in disgrace. We'll not have any of that failure stuff in our family!

No, we didn't! What do you think we did? What have you done in this, or similar, circumstances? We expressed our pride and happiness in her efforts. We rushed to pick her up, hugged her, praised her for trying, and encouraged her to try again. Punishment or criticism would have discouraged her continued efforts.

How did Jessie respond to her failure? Initially she was not a happy child. In fact, she was more than a little upset. But when

Barbara and I comforted, praised, and encouraged her, what did she do? She tried again. Now let's stop and think about this scenario. Jessie tried something for the first time in the presence of the two most important people in her life, and she failed. In a matter of minutes, she was willing to try that same activity again in front of those same people.

I understand that part of her resolve can be attributed to nature, to the fact that our children arrive with the potential and drive to try the things they see large people doing. I am also convinced that the way we large people respond to their efforts, particularly their failures, has an impact on their willingness to continue trying—and on the ultimate success of their efforts. The type of environment that parents create in their homes can support, facilitate, and expedite their children's growth, and one characteristic of such environments is that they are change-friendly.

Now, let's jump ahead fifteen or twenty years and look in on Jessie, who has graduated college, with honors, of course, and has landed a great job in Austin, Texas, where she makes enough money to support her aging parents, one of whom is me…Sorry, I got a little carried away there. Back to Jessie's job.

After completing her initial training, and having been in her job for a while, Jessie believes there are better—more efficient or effective—ways to do the things she's been trained to do; she's found what she believes are better ways. Being blessed with courage and initiative, Jessie decides to give those new ways a try, and she does so in the presence of her boss. Her first efforts are clumsy, mediocre at best. Here's my question: how would you expect Jessie's boss to respond? If this were your company and your boss—or you—what type of response would she get?

Obviously, the responses will vary, and those responses will provide clues about the culture in that organization. If Jessie's initiative is acknowledged and praised, and if the boss then works with her to facilitate improvements in her performance, that's a pretty good indication that she's working in a change-friendly culture.

If, on the other hand, she's admonished for deviating from prescribed practices and warned not to repeat her "indiscretion," what would that tell us about the culture? Change-friendly? Hardly.

Here's an alternative for you to consider, an alternative to the old saying we've associated with playing not to lose, the one that goes like this: "If it ain't broke, don't fix it." For me, this alternative captures the essence of what I mean when I suggest that creating and sustaining change-friendly environments is a requirement for breaking out of the Happily Ever After cycle—and winning. I'm convinced it applies to every type of organization, and it goes like this:

> **If we haven't found a better way,
> it's only because we haven't looked.**

I'm not advocating change for the sake of change. I've said that there are certainly circumstances in which playing "not to lose" (sticking with what we know will work) is appropriate. What I am suggesting is that waiting until something breaks before looking for alternatives (better ways), is a sure way to get "behind the power curve" in organizational settings. The fact that a practice or technique or activity is yielding positive results doesn't eliminate the possibility that alternatives could yield even better results.

Playing to win means not relying on others' mistakes for our success. Playing to win means engaging in a continuous—a relentless—search for better ways, and in order for people to participate actively and effectively in such a search, they must know that their efforts will be supported.

Change-friendly cultures support expanded participation in crucial organizational processes, and leadership behavior is the key driver of such environments. Before people in operational positions will participate actively in the Relentless Search for Better Ways, they must know that the people in positions of leadership in their organizations are willing to consider *and try* alternatives to the status quo.

And that leads us to the third requirement for breaking the Happily Ever After cycle: expanded participation in the Relentless Search for Better Ways.

CHAPTER 4 SUMMARY

- There is often a gap between the culture an organization professes to have and the culture in place.

- The way decisions are made and implemented will reflect some of the fundamental components of an organization's culture.

- Before they can expect broad participation in the Relentless Search for Better Ways, organizational leaders must create and sustain cultures that are change-friendly.

- Change-friendly cultures are ones in which there is widespread willingness to consider and try alternatives to the status quo.

- In change-friendly cultures, questioning the status quo is not only allowed, it is encouraged and expected.

- An organization's culture can encourage playing not to lose by discouraging people from incurring short-term risks.

- The payoff for avoiding short-term risks may be temporary comfort, but the price of that short-term comfort might take the form of greater long-term risks.

- Change-friendly cultures encourage playing to win, based on the premise that if we haven't found a better way, it's only because we haven't looked.

- Setbacks are inevitable, especially in organizations with change-friendly cultures.

- The way people in leadership positions respond to setbacks will determine whether the culture will remain change-friendly or become just another failed experiment.

Chapter 5

Participants in the Search for Better Ways

So far in this book, we've debunked the Happily Ever After myth, and have recognized that accountability is a compelling alternative to victimhood. Finally, we've cut through all the buzzwords and phrases and settled on one, key characteristic of sustainable organizational cultures: they are change-friendly. With all that under our belts, it's time to look at yet another requirement for organizational viability, expanded participation in the Relentless Search for Better Ways.

Not surprisingly, there are two primary groups of people who play key roles in this expanded participation. You've got your "expanders" and "expandees." As you might suspect, the expanders are the people in leadership positions. These are the folks who—before they caught on that expanded participation might be beneficial—held on tightly to the notion that they, and they alone, were qualified and authorized to participate in the Relentless Search for Better Ways.

The other group, the larger of the two, is comprised of the expandees. They are the people whose roles—prior to being expanded—were limited. Hence the need for expansion. The status quo for traditional organizations includes clear distinctions between these two groups and the roles they play in organizational processes.

Enter Bearden, preaching the gospel of expanded participation. Let's take a look at traditional organizations, their separation of powers, and some of the flaws inherent in their approaches.

The Plan From On High

As I mentioned earlier, traditional organizations are hierarchical, with tightly defined roles for people at different levels within the hierarchy. In a typical, hierarchical organization, participation in planning is limited to a relatively few people, usually those in top managerial or executive positions. About once each year, these people go "to the mountaintop"—often disguised as a golf resort—with their retinue of consultants. And while there, they create their strategic plans.

After completing the planning process, they come down and issue the plans to the implementers. The creators then exhort the implementers to "go forth and implement this new and exciting plan we've created for you."

Within a few weeks, many of the creators find themselves frantically contacting motivational speakers, asking for their help in getting their associates to be more enthusiastic in their implementation efforts. Or, they'll contact other consultants, asking for their help in modifying, improving, or tweaking their plans to accommodate some gaps between the plan and its successful implementation out in the real world.

The Relentless Search for Better Ways is a process designed to accomplish and support the following three objectives:

1. Creation: developing actionable plans.
2. Implementation: putting those plans into action.
3. Continuous process improvement: improving the plans based on experiences with implementation.

Conspicuously absent in the first step, creation, and the third step, improvement, are the people whose efforts are absolutely required for organizational success, the implementers. Their participation is extremely important for a variety of reasons. Let's look at a few of them now.

Why Expanders Should "Expand"

Those of you who routinely participate in organizational planning can probably agree with me on several points. First, your success as an organization is influenced, probably determined, by how well your plans actually play out. Second, while you and only a few others may create these plans, their ultimate success is determined by the skill and enthusiasm with which they are implemented. For your plans to succeed, implementers must be committed to putting those plans into action. Third, many—maybe most—of the implementers perform tasks that none of the planners usually perform. Simply stated:

> **Implementers have real-world experience in performing the tasks essential to the success of your plans.**

With all those agreements under our belts, let me go out on a limb here and offer a few opinions and suggestions:

1. Your success is a function of how well you plan, and how well your plans are implemented.
2. If your plans are flawed, even the most spirited implementation efforts will not produce the results you want.
3. Even if your plans are flawless, unless they are effectively, efficiently, and enthusiastically implemented, they'll remain academic achievements with little or no practical value.
4. Can I get an "amen" here?

The skills, talents, and commitment of implementers are essential to your success. One way to obtain their commitment to implementing plans is to include them—their skills, talents, and perspectives—when creating those plans. You'll also find that the quality of your plans will improve when you expand implementers' participation in their creation.

Think about this:

1. These folks perform tasks that you don't perform.
2. They have more experience, expertise, and real-world perspective on what can and can't be done.

So, don't you think their participation in creating plans will:

1. Increase the viability of those plans?
2. Reduce the time needed to resolve misunderstandings?
3. Close the gaps between the plans (theory) and their implementation (action)?

Inviting implementers to participate in planning will not only enhance their commitment to executing those plans, it will also send a clear message about expanding the boundaries of their accountability for the plan's ultimate success.

A Voice, Not a Vote!

You expanders, take a deep breath and relax. Don't worry, I'll get to the expandees soon, so don't think this entire chapter will be devoted to all the things you've got to do.

I understand that many organizations have moved toward less-hierarchical structures with fewer bureaucratic divisions. What I'm suggesting is that you take a good look at how decisions are made and implemented in your organization, with an eye toward expanding the roles that people are currently playing.

The type of decision making I'm referring to in this example involves the creation of organizational plans. How those plans are created and implemented will reveal much about your organizational culture. Including implementers in the creative process is characteristic of a culture that is, indeed, change-friendly. As "expanders," you must not only invite them to participate, you must demonstrate your willingness to consider their input.

Before you throw up your hands and conclude that I'm encouraging you to abdicate your role in creating plans, and your accountability for their viability, let me point out a distinction I see at work. I encourage you to ensure that implementers have a *voice* in the creative process. However, I'm not suggesting that you turn that process into an exercise in democracy. The distinction here is between giving people a voice and giving them a vote, and I vote for the former.

> **When inviting people to participate in creating organizational plans, make sure you clearly explain the specific role(s) you're asking them to play and the areas in which their input is needed.**

As to my earlier "golf resort" analogy about strategic planning, please don't get the impression that I was thumbing my nose at that process. I wasn't. I understand the value of developing organizational strategies, and I also understand that trying to involve *everyone* in that process is not only unrealistic, it's unnecessary.

However, translating strategies into tactics, actions, processes, and activities calls for expanded participation in the planning process. It is at this stage that implementers' input—their opinions, suggestions, questions, and even challenges—can dramatically improve the quality of the plans and ease the transition from planning to action.

With that, why don't you expanders take a short break. Now it's time to shift our focus to those of you who will be encouraged to play additional roles, the expandees.

Before sharing my rationale for why you expandees should participate actively in the Relentless Search for Better Ways, let me share with you a composite review of my experiences with organizations struggling to expand participants' roles.

The "Growing Pains" of Expanded Participation

Several years ago the Texas Legislature mandated something called "Site-Based Decision Making" for public school districts. In a nutshell, this legislation directed district administrators and school boards to involve classroom teachers, parents, and members of the community in decisions about curriculum, teaching methods, and other educational issues. Before this legislation was passed, such decisions were the exclusive domain of the administrators and school boards.

It's also interesting to note that before the legislation, many classroom teachers and organizations representing them had lobbied, rightfully I think, for inclusion in the decision-making process. So, the legislation passed, and as with most changes, this one was met with rejoicing in some quarters and much wailing and gnashing of teeth in others. We were off and running with a real-world example of expanded participation in the Relentless Search for Better Ways.

As the "new" wore off, the reality began to set in, and many districts began trying to implement the new approach. Not surprisingly, many of them were unsure just how to proceed. While plenty of administrators and board members had solicited teachers' and parents' input, many others had not. And while some teachers had participated in the decision-making process in their departments, on their campuses, or in their districts, many more had not. These professionals were willing to function as expanders and expandees, but they weren't sure *how to proceed*.

Happily, I was contacted by several districts and by the statewide association of school boards and invited to do training and help the parties implement this new version of decision-making.

Here are two problems some of the parties were having in their attempts to implement site-based decision making:

1. Some administrators weren't sure how to facilitate expanded participation.
2. Some teachers weren't sure how, or even if, they wanted to participate.

The administrators and board members had become quite comfortable in the role of decision makers, and most were good people who were trying, in good faith, to do what they'd been hired and trained to do. They made decisions. Period.

The teachers, on the other hand, had lobbied for inclusion in the decision-making process. They recognized that, as implementers, they were held accountable for executing plans, policies, and procedures created and issued to them by people who did not spend their days in classrooms full of students. They were impacted by the decisions those administrators and board members made, and they were ultimately responsible for the success or failure of the district's education plans. By golly, they wanted a voice in creating them. Can you blame them?

So along came the legislation, site-based decision-making became the law of the land, and the teachers were given a voice. Just as the administrators had become familiar with their role as decision makers, the teachers had become familiar—if not particularly comfortable—with their role as decision implementers. But in many instances, the teachers' discomfort with implementing others' decisions was not as pronounced as their discomfort when faced with the prospect of actually participating in decision-making.

The two problems were that administrators weren't sure how to facilitate expanded participation, and teachers weren't sure how to participate. So what happened? In some districts, not much. After dancing around with the new mandates, some districts simply stayed with the status quo. Input may have been solicited, but the same people made the same decisions they probably would have made anyway. In fact, some of these decisions were probably made before input was ever solicited. Many teachers expressed grave misgivings about participating in decision-making, fearing that their lack of experience would lead them to make bad decisions. Those teachers opted to function only as implementers of decisions made by others. Opportunities for improving the decision-making process—and the quality of decisions—were squandered.

That certainly wasn't the case in all, or even most districts, where the parties rolled up their sleeves and set about learning new skills. Administrators became competent facilitators, and teachers provided invaluable input based on their experiences as implementers. The quality of the decisions made in those districts, and the effectiveness with which they are being implemented stand as proof that expanded participation has tremendous potential value.

There were and are payoffs for those districts, but the changes that have produced those payoffs were not made without lots of effort. All parties had to learn new skills, and that included grappling with the mediocrity that characterized their early efforts. To their credit, most professional educators have opted to do so, and their efforts are positively impacting the quality of education in our public schools. This example reinforces the importance of perseverance—*after the "new" wears off.*

Why Participate?

Earlier in this book, I talked about the Happily Ever After myth. Here's another myth we should consider: "employment for life." Do you remember that one? For years—actually, for generations—people in our country were convinced that if they went to work for the right organization, they were guaranteed employment for life. Until fairly recently, that myth seemed to be a fact, and then we entered the age of "corporate re-engineering" and "downsizing." What happened to employment for life?

May I be so bold as to suggest that employment for life, as an expectation, has fallen prey to the phenomenon I described earlier in this book:

> **The people and situations in our lives change.
> As they change, so do the requirements
> for our success.**

The people and situations *have* changed. More global competition, more price pressures, demand for more efficiencies, shorter product shelf lives, rapid technological innovations—all these changes have created a job market in which employers' requirements for success have changed. Companies must be able to devote more resources to initiatives such as R&D and marketing. That means that fewer resources, e.g., dollars, can be devoted to personnel.

Employment for life? I don't think so. Most employers must be able to justify every dollar invested, and more of their dollars are tied up in people than any other line item. The people they employ must provide sufficient value to justify their continued employment. Employment for life has become *employability* for life. Participation in the Relentless Search for Better Ways, once a discretionary activity, is becoming a requirement for employability—and employment.

I'm talking primarily to you expandees, those of you whose roles have been limited to implementing the decisions made by others and meeting the standards they've established. As employment for life has been replaced by employability for life, you may not have detected any change in your roles. You still function primarily as an implementer. No one in your organization has invited you to participate in decision making, so you assume that as long as you perform adequately in your implementer role, your job is secure. Bad assumption.

Regardless of the role you play in your organization, I suggest you consider two conclusions I've drawn from the "downsizing craze."

The first one goes like this:

1. **Your value to your employer is not determined exclusively by how well you perform the tasks listed on your job description.** Those tasks are obviously important, but performing them proficiently is no longer enough. Yes, you were hired to perform those tasks, and your performance evaluations

focus almost exclusively on how well you perform them, so your proficiency at performing those tasks is clearly important. What I'm saying is that the skill with which you perform those tasks is just the "ante." You probably won't get many extra points for performing your assigned tasks well.

If your performance is superior to that of others performing the same tasks in your organization, you'll probably have some degree of job security. Unless your performance meets the minimum standards, you'll probably have no job security. Your job security, or employability, is impacted by how well you perform your assigned tasks, *but your performance of those tasks is not the only measure of your value to your employer.*

You've got to believe that when one American company lays off 70,000 people in one fell swoop, some of those unemployed people performed their assigned tasks pretty darn well.

Here's my second conclusion:

2. **Your value to your employer is also determined by your ability and your willingness to participate actively in the Relentless Search for Better Ways.** In addition to performing your assigned tasks well, *you must continuously look for ways to perform them better.* Meeting the standards set by others is fine, as far as it goes. But it just doesn't go far enough. You must look for ways to raise those standards and then meet or exceed them.

A New Look at Performance Evaluations

What I'm talking about here is continuous performance improvement, something that is obviously important to organizations everywhere. In fact, most organizations do use a process designed to drive such improvements. What I'm talking about here are performance appraisals done on some sort of regular basis for employees, and in our Relentless Search for Better Ways, the performance appraisal process is a prime candidate for improvement.

In the conventional approach, there are two primary participants in the performance-appraisal process. There are the evaluators—usually managers or supervisors—and the people whose performance is being evaluated, who I'll refer to as employees. My idea for a better way involves expanding the roles played by employees.

Before launching into my thoughts about how to improve it, let me go on record as endorsing the formal performance-appraisal process. As I see it, the process provides benefits for both groups of participants.

Employees benefit from knowing what their managers or supervisors think about their performance. Employees understand that evaluators' perceptions can impact their career progression and even their job security. They have a right to know what those perceptions are. Since the objective of performance appraisals is to facilitate improved performance, employees must know which areas of their performance evaluators think need improvement. If they aren't aware of areas in which improvements are needed, what's the likelihood that they'll put effort into improving those areas?

Evaluators benefit from knowing that they have to provide accurate and relevant feedback on all employees' performance. That's not to say that all evaluators are conscientious in monitoring employees' performance, but for those who are, the formal performance appraisal process reminds them that focusing exclusively on the efforts of a few employees won't work.

If you've ever been responsible for the performance of a group of people, then you know how easy it is to fixate on certain people in the group. For example, in most organizations there are the top performers, the chronic underperformers, and the folks in the middle, whose performance is average. And which group is most easily and frequently overlooked? It's the midrange employees. And which group seems to get most of evaluators' attention? It's the chronic underperformers.

Ignoring the midrange folks in deference to chronic underperformers is a big mistake, and there are at least two reasons to avoid making it. First, there are (hopefully) far more average performers than there are chronic underperformers, so if you ignore them, you're ignoring the majority of your employees. Second, which of the two groups, average performers or chronic underperformers, would you expect to respond more favorably to performance-improvement efforts? I'm sure you'll agree that the latter group has probably resisted other attempts, while the first group, the average performers, may have gotten too little attention in the past. It sure seems to me that the middle group offers the best opportunity for facilitating performance improvements. Knowing that they are expected to provide timely, thoughtful performance appraisals for *all* employees reminds evaluators to spend the time necessary to do so.

OK, so the formal performance appraisal process has plenty of merit, and because it does, it's a process we should target in our Relentless Search for Better Ways. As I see it, there is one modification we can make to the process, a change that will transform performance *appraisal* into performance *improvement*.

Here's how the performance-appraisal process works in most organizations:

1. Managers or supervisors do the evaluations by conducting a formal performance appraisal for each employee, usually once per year.

2. In their appraisals, evaluators share some variation of the following information with employees:

- Their overall perceptions of how the employee is performing.
- Areas of strength in their performance.
- Areas in which improvements are needed.
- Suggestions for making those improvements.

The employees are then expected to act on the recommendations made by the evaluators. While there may be circumstances in which evaluators do aggressive follow-up, e.g., for employees on some form of probation, most employees can expect their next performance appraisal in a year.

Let's start with frequency: most employees can expect performance appraisals one time each year. If that's the case, how often would you expect the average employee to think much about improving his or her performance? I'm guessing the answer is about one time each year, and that would be either just prior to, or immediately following the annual performance appraisal. In today's rapidly changing organizational environments, is once per year enough? How successful are individuals and organizations going to be if they only consider making improvements one time each year? And yet, the message being sent to employees in most organizations is that they are only expected to think about their performance and ways to improve it once a year.

Now let's look at the roles participants play in the conventional approach to performance appraisal: evaluators and employees. Employees rely—sometimes exclusively—on evaluators to determine how they can improve their performance. Consider this: most employees perform tasks that their evaluators do not perform. OK, the evaluators may have performed those tasks—or some variation on those tasks—earlier in their careers, but they do not perform them any longer. So what that means is that we have evaluators telling employees how to improve tasks that the evaluators do not perform.

I understand that having a different perspective on those tasks can help evaluators see things that the employees do not see. Remember, I'm a big fan of the formal performance-appraisal process. What I'm lobbying for is an expansion of the roles being played by employees. Instead of relying exclusively on evaluators to offer suggestions for how to improve their performance, why shouldn't employees be expected to come up with some ideas of their own? Instead of waiting for the formal performance appraisal (usually an annual event), why shouldn't employees engage in more frequent or continuous scrutiny of the things they're doing, how they're doing them, and the results they're producing? I'm convinced that the reason those things don't happen is because no one is facilitating such a process.

The better way I'm talking about here is a fundamental shift in how performance appraisals are perceived and performed. Instead of a once-per-year event, performance appraisal—and performance improvement—should be seen as an ongoing process.

> **Instead of just doing performance appraisals, evaluators should facilitate a process by which employees become far more active in evaluating and improving their own performance.**

Employees, the people who perform the tasks essential to organizational success, have the experience and expertise necessary to identify viable alternatives to the status quo where those tasks are concerned. Evaluators, the people who—theoretically, at least—possess the leadership skills necessary to do so, must expand the roles employees play in the appraisal and improvement process. It's a better way, just waiting to be found.

Expanded participation in the Relentless Search for Better Ways includes searching for better ways to perform your assigned tasks or for better tasks to perform, ones that will produce better results and deliver more value. Since you perform those tasks every day, you're in the best position to figure out better ways to perform them or to identify better tasks to perform. Waiting for somebody else to find better ways is a sure way to limit your value and your employability.

Enthusiasm Delivers and Redelivers

I've said that your value is determined, not just by how well you perform your assigned tasks, but also by your ability and willingness to participate actively in the Relentless Search for Better Ways. Your ability to participate is determined by your capacity to think, learn, and perform. Some people have more ability to participate; their ideas, questions, and efforts will be more valuable than those of others with less ability.

Willingness is another matter. People who are willing to participate, who enthusiastically engage in the Relentless Search for Better Ways, can deliver value in several ways.

First, their commitment to the process will lead them to contribute their best ideas and put forth their best efforts. They'll deliver more of their potential value than those who are not committed and do not participate, or who participate half-heartedly.

Second, by their efforts, they'll serve as positive role models for others, reinforcing the efforts of managers and other facilitators. Because of their example, more people will be willing to participate in the search. Finally, more and more people will begin to discover compelling alternatives to the way they've performed their assigned tasks. They may even identify better tasks to perform. The culture will become more and more change-friendly, and organizational effectiveness and efficiency will improve dramatically.

Unfortunately, the reverse is also true. I said earlier that limited ability limits a person's value as an employee. Here's how I see this limitation in ability and willingness coming into play:

> **Limited ability limits value.**
> **Limited willingness *reduces* value.**

Think about it. If you're a staff member who has the ability to participate in the search for better ways, but you're unwilling to do so, can't you see how you've effectively reduced your value and your employability? No? OK, see if this makes sense.

As an employer, I must try to get maximum value from every dollar I spend. Every staff member must contribute sufficient value to justify the investment I'm making in him or her. If you have the ability to participate, but you're unwilling to do so, I'm incurring actual costs—and opportunity costs. The actual costs include things like salary, benefits, etc. The opportunity costs are the things I could be getting if I was paying *somebody else* your salary, benefits, etc. In this case, the opportunity costs I'm incurring are the ideas I could be getting from someone who was willing to participate in the Relentless Search for Better Ways.

Here's another way unwillingness reduces value. I have seldom encountered people who were *silently* unwilling. When I invite people to participate in the Relentless Search for Better Ways, to suggest, consider, and try alternatives to the status quo, the people who are most unwilling are usually quite vocal about their unwillingness. Remember what I said about the value of people who might have limited ability, but are willing to try. They provide value in at least the three ways I listed. But the folks who are vocally unwilling reduce their value by negatively influencing others. It's bad enough if they're unwilling, but when they "recruit" others to their "cause," they've negatively impacted the entire process. Their value is not just limited, it's reduced—and believe me—so is their employability.

Finally, facilitators, the people who are attempting to expand participation in the Relentless Search for Better Ways, to encourage people to engage in that search, will probably devote a disproportionate amount of their time and energy trying to convince unwilling people to participate. They'll also expend time and energy trying to mitigate the negative impact on others of these unwilling "crusaders." People with limited willingness reduce their value by creating obstacles and problems that require facilitators' time and energy.

Let the Search Begin

So there you have it, my impassioned plea for expanding participation in the Relentless Search for Better Ways.

Enough with the theory, let's get down to some practical ideas for how to facilitate and participate in the search. Surely at this point no one could possibly quarrel with my logic or my position on this important process: organizations must engage in a Relentless Search for Better Ways, and that search must include participation by people at all levels within those organizations.

Chapter 5 Summary

- The Relentless Search for Better Ways is a process for creating, implementing and fine-tuning actionable plans for achieving individual and organizational success.

- People whose efforts are essential to effectively and enthusiastically implementing plans should participate in creating those plans.

- Including implementers in the creative process is characteristic of a culture that is, indeed, change-friendly.

- When inviting people to participate in creating organizational plans, make sure you clearly explain to them the specific roles you're asking them to play and the areas in which their input is needed.

- Our value as employees is not determined exclusively by how well we perform our assigned tasks.

- Our value as employees is also determined by our ability and willingness to participate actively in the Relentless Search for Better Ways.

- Expanded participation in the Relentless Search for Better Ways includes the search for better ways to perform your assigned tasks, or for better tasks to perform.

- Limited ability to participate limits participants' value.

- Limited willingness to participate *reduces* non-participants' value.

CHAPTER 6

Searching for Better Ways

As I see it, the Relentless Search for Better Ways is a four-step process. Let's take a look at the steps so you can get busy adapting them for your outfit. For you visually oriented people, and for those of you who just might be ready for something besides words, here's a model of the Relentless Search for Better Ways.

Together, the 4 steps represent a cycle. In the following pages, I will describe each of the steps. As I do so, you might find it helpful to refer back to the model to see the context in which that step occurs.

The Relentless Search for Better Ways
A Model for Collaborative Processes

STEP 1: DELIBERATE
- Thoughtful input (think and share)
- Inquiry-driven (ask and listen)
- Whats, whys, hows

STEP 2: DECIDE
- Choose/bless
- Define success
- Create plan

STEP 3: IMPLEMENT
- Ideas into action
- Time for deliberation is over (for now)
- Team players vs. team members

STEP 4: IMPROVE
- Finding better ways
- Processes and outcomes
- Remember, apply, forget

Step 1: Deliberate

I understand that the word "deliberate" can be either an adjective, as in "John is a very deliberate person," or a verb, à la "Let's deliberate!" It's the latter form I'm using here. I'm talking about the act of deliberating, and this first step is where I would expect to see maximum participation in the Relentless Search for Better Ways.

When I suggest deliberation, what actions do you envision? When I ask audiences this question, the first response I almost always get is some variation on "discussion." To most of us, deliberation is discussing, debating, or brainstorming, and most often our efforts are focused on a specific issue or topic. We would expect people engaged in deliberation to share their ideas and/or ask questions. We'd also expect them to try to understand others' positions and recommendations. Understanding requires that other communication skill, listening.

> Deliberation is some combination
> of sharing, listening to,
> and considering information and positions
> on the issues being addressed.

As promised, I'll share ideas for how the facilitators and the active participants in the deliberation can contribute to its effectiveness. You'll recall my labels for these two groups: "expanders," the facilitators, and "expandees," the participants. I'll start with the facilitators.

Advance Notice

Effective deliberations, ones that yield worthwhile, measurable results, will probably not occur spontaneously. That's not to say that people don't spend plenty of time talking with each other about organizational issues, because they do. These "intramural" discussions—often characterized by complaining— seldom produce much in the way of workable solutions to problems. As facilitators, your first step toward ensuring effective deliberations is to extend invitations, to actively solicit people's participation in the process. And when extending invitations, you'll take a giant step toward improving the quality of participants' input by giving sufficient advance notice.

When you invite people to participate in a deliberation, or whatever you want to call it—exchange of ideas, brainstorming, planning—you should do so far enough in advance to allow them to prepare. Encourage people to take the time in advance to *think* about the issues or topics you've invited them to help address. On "game day," when the participants begin the sharing, listening, and considering that comprise these deliberations, I'm guessing that you'd prefer to have thoughtful, concise, and reasonable input. While there are no absolute guarantees, I'm convinced that, when given advance notice and encouraged to think about the issues, participants' input will be more to the point and easier to listen to and consider. Giving advance notice will help you and your associates accomplish more in less time, thereby improving the effectiveness and efficiency of your deliberations.

I'll have some suggestions for how you participants can use the time you're given to prepare and participate effectively. But for now, let me suggest that when you're invited to participate, make sure you understand the issues to be addressed and the objectives for the deliberation. If the person extending the invitation doesn't offer that information, ask for it. You're being asked to spend your time and energy participating in this process, so you have every reason to expect some return on your investment.

Here are three things to remember when inviting people to participate in deliberation:

1. Clearly define the issues to be addressed.

2. Establish specific goals for the deliberation.

3. Give participants advance notice so that they'll have time to formulate their thoughts.

Ask and Listen

I've suggested that deliberation includes sharing, listening, and considering. When people are engaged in good-faith discussions, there will be a healthy mix of these activities. An absence of any of them will detract significantly from the effectiveness of the process.

The fact is, few of those activities will occur spontaneously. If a CEO issued a memo stating that collaborative decision making was something she believed to be important, would you expect deliberations to suddenly break out all over the organization? Would people stop whatever they were doing and seek out other people with whom they could deliberate for the purpose of making some decisions? Hardly.

Like teamwork and business development, deliberation doesn't "just happen"; facilitation is required. Facilitating effective deliberations requires proficiency in two basic communication skills: asking and listening.

Here's my short course on the importance of asking questions and of listening to people's responses when facilitating deliberations:

Asking questions is how you initiate deliberation. Listening is how you sustain the process.

Asking questions is an excellent technique for initiating deliberation, and it is a tool I recommend for facilitators. Listening is how facilitators can sustain the process. Participants are more willing to continue sharing their ideas when they know somebody is actually listening. The facilitator, then, encourages sharing by listening. But that's not the end of the good news.

Think back, now, on your recent experiences with group discussions. Regardless of the setting or participants, I'm guessing that your experiences have been similar to mine and most other people's. Let's look at some common characteristics of our experiences and see how effective facilitation might have improved the process—and the results. Let's see, what's a good one to start with? OK, how about groups in which the facilitator dominates. Ever been in one like that?

Too often, the people in the best positions to function as facilitators turn out to be "dominators." They call meetings or get a group together to "discuss" issues and ostensibly to get those people's input. But does it ever seem to you that the only input they're really seeking is the group's blessing of their ideas? They've read or heard somebody say that including others in decision making is good for morale. So they're willing to spend a few minutes pretending to be interested in what others think. Hey, anything for better morale, right? Do I have to tell you that such a charade doesn't really work?

Facilitators, take note: If you've already made up your mind as to how we're going to proceed, I'd rather that you just announce your decision rather than insisting that I waste my time in your "make-believe deliberation."

If you are in a position of authority, and if you've pretty much decided how to address an issue, you still might want to bounce your ideas off some people. That being the case, tell them what you're asking them to do. If you are pretty sure how to proceed, tell them, and then invite them to critique your idea. Needless to say, if you have a reputation as someone who only wants to hear from people who agree with you, you probably aren't going to get many tough questions or suggested alternatives to your ideas. People will tell you what they think you want to hear.

However, if you've created a change-friendly culture based on a willingness to consider and try alternatives to the status quo—

even when the status quo consists of your ideas—you can get some potentially valuable input. But even in this type of environment, you've got to ask. And then you've got to listen.

Here's something to remember:

> **If you aren't willing to listen,
> don't bother asking.**

Here's another characteristic of "pseudo-deliberation." It's one we've all been involved in, especially those of us with opinionated coworkers or family members (is there any other kind?). Everybody talks, usually at the same time, and nobody listens. Participants leave with the same opinions they came with—theirs. Granted, many of these people probably have some good ideas. But in many of these "word fights," the folks with the best ideas are often the quietest. I mean, how could they hope to compete with people who believe that the value of their input is directly proportional to the volume with which they share it?

In these free-for-alls, there's no shortage of ideas. Nor are participants unwilling to share them. However, unless the parties are willing to listen and consider others' ideas, the chances of the deliberation producing anything of value are remote. Productive deliberation requires participants who are not only eager to share their ideas, but also willing to listen.

Asking questions encourages others to share. Listening and trying to understand others' input is one way to indicate willingness to consider what they're saying, and to encourage them to continue sharing. When facilitators listen to a participant's input, they're also sending a message about what they expect other participants to do. When someone is speaking, others are expected to listen to and consider what the speaker is saying.

As for those of you whose input is being sought, bring your ideas and questions to the deliberation, and don't be shy about sharing them. Just don't forget that your participation includes listening to and considering the ideas, questions, and positions of others. Apparently many of us believe that if we listen to people without interrupting them, they'll think we agree with them. God knows, we wouldn't want them to think that. So how do we avoid that potentially hazardous possibility? We jump right in whenever we hear anything we don't like. I mean, if we don't rebut it as soon as we hear it, we might forget to do so—or we might forget some clever comeback we've thought of.

This brings us to my final example of behavior that sabotages the best-intentioned deliberation. How many of us *really* listen to what others are saying? Come on, be honest. Let me ask it another way. How many of you can think of five people in your lives who listen carefully to you when you speak? I'm talking about five people who discontinue whatever they're doing, look at you, and focus one hundred percent of their attention on what you're saying, people who work hard to ensure that they understand not just what you're saying, but what you mean. How many of you can think of five such people? OK, how many of you can think of one?

Understandably, my wife, Barbara, comes to mind. She would be quick to say that I am probably the single most accomplished listener she's ever encountered. And then she'd say that Texas isn't hot in the summertime and snakes are cuddly animals. Barbara does come to mind—as a listener. Whether it's our children or me, when we speak to her, Barbara listens to understand. It makes me crazy sometimes when she stops me in mid-delivery to ask for clarification on something I've just said. But she's doing exactly what I would expect good listeners to do. She's seeking verification or clarification, instead of relying on assumptions.

We've agreed that listening and considering are important activities in the deliberative process. Before I can really consider a point of view or opinion, I must understand it. In order to understand it, I must listen with that objective in mind. Listening to understand may require me to periodically ask the other person to pause so that I can verify or clarify what I've understood up to that point. That's real listening. Let's compare that to what usually happens.

We assume that if others are silent when we're speaking, they're listening. Here's a hot flash: *they're probably not*. If we speak for more than just a few seconds, especially if the opinion we're sharing differs from the opinions held by the other parties, we can be pretty sure that they aren't really listening. So, what are they doing? They're thinking of clever ways to dismantle our opinion, to show us up for the idiots we must be for disagreeing with them. They can't wait for us to come up for air so they can pounce. How much of what we say have they heard? Just enough to know that our opinion is different from theirs. How well do they understand our opinion? Well enough to know that it's different from theirs and, therefore, we must be idiots. If we continue for too long after they've formulated their devastating rebuttals, they'll just jump in and talk right along with us—and may the windiest win.

Again, effective deliberation includes sharing, listening, and considering ideas and questions. Good faith on the part of all participants is essential. When facilitators model such behavior, they're encouraging others to follow their lead. The quality of the deliberative process and the results it produces will reflect their effectiveness as facilitators.

Beyond Perceived Limits

By expanding the search for better ways; specifically, by including implementers in this important first step—deliberation—we will accomplish at least two objectives. First, we'll validate their importance to the ultimate success of the process we're planning. Their participation increases their ownership of, and commitment to, the plan and its implementation. Since their efforts are essential to producing the results the plan is designed to deliver, I'd say their ownership and commitment are mighty important, wouldn't you?

Second, implementers' input can dramatically improve the quality and implementability (yet another new word) of the plan. I am convinced that most people work below their potential. Few of us produce at one hundred percent of our capacity in any area of our lives. OK, surely politicians perform pretty close to one hundred percent of their "spin potential"—at least we all hope so. But with that one exception, most people function well below their potential, both physically and mentally. That phenomenon will have an impact on the search for better ways. Fortunately, there are some things facilitators can do to elevate the level of participation and the quality of its finished product—the plan.

Think back on times in your life when you've had to stretch, either physically or mentally. Surely there have been situations in which you've found it necessary to go beyond what you'd thought were your limits. While you're coming up with some examples of your own, I'll share one of mine. As I do—and as you reflect back on yours—try to recall the "triggers," the things that caused you to go beyond your "limits."

A Marine Corps "Trigger"

Ah, the Marine Corps, a veritable storehouse of experiential learning. Let's see, the subject is stretching, going beyond what we believed were our limits, right? So do you think the Marine Corps places much stock in that sort of thing? Surely you recognize a rhetorical question when you see one. So, where to begin? How about November 1967?

As an officer candidate, I had become convinced that the objective of the training was to kill us all. I had become accustomed to daily doses of "stretching." One particularly difficult activity was called the Speed March Reaction Course.

After being commissioned as Marine officers, we would be required to make decisions—many of them life-or-death decisions—under stressful conditions. Remember, this was 1967. One objective of our training was to put us in scenarios where we were required to make decisions under stress. Since shooting at us with live ammunition was discouraged by the kinder, gentler Marine Corps, our trainers created stress using rigorous physical exercise, tight time limits, and loud noises. Their screaming at us comes to mind.

So, the Speed March Reaction Course exercise began with our donning every piece of gear we possessed, including: steel helmets, packs loaded with ballast, belts with full canteens and ammunition attached, and our rifles. After ensuring that all of us were suitably weighed down and generally uncomfortable—a prerequisite to every Marine training exercise—our instructors led us on a brisk three-mile run over the Hill Course, affectionately known as the "Hell" Course. I'll let you draw your own conclusions about the terrain, but be sure to include the word "steep" in your mental description.

The run ended, mercifully, at a series of obstacles we hadn't seen before. With no recovery time, we were dispatched, in four-man teams, to our first obstacle. Upon arriving at the obstacle, we were greeted by two trainers who designated one member of the team as the leader for that obstacle. The leaders were given minutes to develop and implement a plan for successfully negotiating the obstacle, for getting all team members, with our gear, across the obstacle, ready to fight.

Each of us had a turn as leader, with different obstacles and different trainers. And each of us made plenty of mistakes that the cheerful trainers were happy to point out to us. Each of us also learned something very important, something that came in handy a few months later in Vietnam.

> **We learned that when necessary, we can perform, mentally and physically, beyond what we'd thought were our limits.**

For most of us then, and most of us today, our "limits" were, and are, well below our true capacity.

Other "Triggers"

Now, let's get back to your examples and my question about the "triggers," the things that caused you to push up to and beyond your "limits." If your experiences have been anything like mine, at least one of the reasons you've pushed yourself was because people you respected expected it. They conveyed their confidence in your ability to do more. In essence, they believed in you while you were still developing your belief in yourself. They may have done things you didn't like, and they may have said things you didn't want to hear, but they also gave you a precious gift. They helped you expand your belief in what you could do.

As facilitators of the deliberative process, you have opportunities to encourage people to stretch, to make contributions beyond what they and others may have seen as their limits. When asking for participants' input, do not be timid about what you ask for. In fact, stand by to be pleasantly surprised at the quality of what participants contribute when you nudge them beyond their "limits."

To help you in your role as facilitators, I've provided a three-word checklist for the information you ask participants to share in your deliberations:

1. Whats.
2. Whys.
3. Hows.

Whats

In deliberations, one of the things we're looking for is participants' thoughts about *what* might prove to be better ways. Here are a couple of examples of these "whats."

If the objective of the deliberation is to identify areas to improve, the whats would be those *areas* participants see as viable candidates for such improvements. If the areas needing improvement have been selected, and the objective is to identify alternative processes within those areas, the alternative *processes* would be the whats.

In either scenario, the whats are important, but they're only the starting points in the Relentless Search for Better Ways. Without demeaning their significance, coming up with a list of the whats doesn't really require participants to do much stretching. Think about it. Can't you recall times—usually late on Friday afternoons—when people have dropped in on you or e-mailed you with ideas about areas that need to be improved or specific changes they think you should make? Hey, they'll have no problem coming up with the whats. After reading this, you'll have no problem encouraging them to do some long-overdue stretching.

Whys

Back to the premise I shared with you earlier:

> **People tend to perform up to or down to the expectations of others, especially the expectations of others they look up to.**

If, as facilitators, all you ask (expect) people to contribute are whats, then that's pretty much what you'll get. A mistake many facilitators make is thinking that's all those people are capable of contributing. The truth is, when you expect and ask more from them, you'll get more—from some of them. In fact, you'll get more from more of them than you would have expected. But in the real world, you won't get more from *all* of them. Sorry. Wish you would, but you won't. But just because you won't get more from all of them is hardly justification for not asking for more from *any* of them.

Here's an interesting ditty I picked up somewhere along the way: ask for what you want, take what you get and work on the difference.

When participants identify areas where they think improvements are needed, *ask them why*. When participants suggest specific changes to existing processes, *ask them why they believe their alternatives would prove more effective*. By asking them to explain their rationale, you're encouraging them to think beyond where they might otherwise have. I'm not suggesting that you challenge or confront them, especially early in the process, when they still need convincing that you're genuinely interested in their ideas and that it's safe to say what they really think. What I am suggesting is that you express curiosity about—and genuine interest in—the rationale behind their whats. Doing so will yield at least two benefits.

First, when asked in a nonadversarial, nonconfrontational way, such a question will reinforce your regard for their opinions. Think about how that will influence their participation. When you believe that someone is genuinely interested in—and has regard for—your opinions, aren't you more willing to share them? I'm guessing the answer is yes, and participants in your deliberative process will probably respond in the same way.

Second, it will enhance the quality of their input. When you ask them, "Why?" you'll provoke more thought. When they stretch themselves mentally, they'll offer up suggestions, or even questions, that contribute more to workable plans for finding and implementing better ways.

Hows

Hey, don't stop now, you're on a roll! Now that you've demonstrated confidence in participants bringing more to the table, take it to the next level. So far, they've identified the areas for improvement or specific changes (their whats) and their reasons for selecting those areas or recommending those changes (their whys). Let's not call it a day just yet.

In keeping with our premise about people holding more cards than they've shown, or having more capacity than they've used, I want you to ask for more. When they've offered up suggestions for areas to improve and their rationale for those suggestions, ask for their ideas about *how* to improve those areas. When they suggest specific changes to make, ask them *how* they would go about making those changes.

Remember, these are people who work every day in the areas you're discussing, so you should be able to rely on them for ideas about specific changes that would represent better ways in those areas. You should also rely on their rationale, the benefits they associate with addressing specific areas or making specific changes, and their ideas for how to effect those changes.

Deliberation can contribute significantly to the quality of the plans you create. By including implementers and by encouraging them to participate at higher levels, you'll improve the quality of the plans you'll ultimately develop, and you'll enhance participants' commitment to their implementation. Way to deliberate!

Before moving to Step 2 of the Relentless Search for Better Ways Model, let's look at an example of deliberation in action.

Deliberation: A Real-World Example

Back in Chapter 2, I used a title insurance industry example to illustrate the steps in my Happily Ever After cycle. When the refinance boom began to play out, the market for closing services began to change. And so did the requirements for my clients' success.

Instead of relying on business to come to them—as it had during the boom—title companies had to become more proactive in their business development efforts. During the boom, homeowners flocked to lenders to refinance their mortgages, and the lenders flocked to title companies to have these new transactions closed. As the volume of refinance business declined, title companies had to actively sell their services to the real estate community.

As in most industries, title companies' sales processes must produce two important results: retain existing customers and win new ones. The two groups of title company personnel with opportunities to produce those results are the closers, who deliver the service to their customers, and the salespeople, who convince prospective customers to use their company's services. One of the challenges the title companies faced was getting closers re-engaged in the selling process. Branch managers were charged with the task of facilitating a process for doing so, and deliberation was the first step many of them used.

Instead of directing the closers to begin performing specific sales-related tasks, the branch managers took a more collaborative approach. They invited closers to participate in discussions about the changing market for their services and the actions they (closers) could take to help ensure a steady stream of business in that market. Branch managers drove the deliberative process with inquiry, asking closers for their perceptions, opinions, and suggestions.

The first order of business for the branch managers was to obtain closers' agreement that the market was, indeed, changing and that the real estate community would be their primary source of business for the foreseeable future. After accomplishing that objective, the branch managers then asked closers to identify sales-related tasks they could perform, going forward. Here are some of the ideas that emerged from their deliberations.

Since closers have direct contact with current customers, they chose to focus their selling efforts on keeping those customers. The salespeople would retain primary responsibility for winning new customers. The closers agreed to be available to help the salespeople with their "hunting" when needed, but their top priority would be to ensure that they understood and met or exceeded their current customers' expectations.

After determining where closers would focus their selling efforts, branch managers asked them for more specific information, including the sales-related activities each closer would perform (whats), their rationale for selecting those activities (whys), and their plans for performing them (hows). They were off and running.

Including closers in the process of determining the sales-related activities they would perform and developing their plans for doing so paid off in a couple of ways.

First, it dramatically reduced the "push-back" factor. When people are ordered or directed to perform tasks—especially tasks with which they're already uncomfortable—they'll probably resist. When the branch managers asked closers for their ideas, and when they actually listened to their responses, they turned what could have been an adversarial process into one that was collaborative.

Second, the plans that emerged had a much better chance of yielding positive results. Since the closers were more comfortable with the activities they committed to performing, they were far more inclined to keep their commitments—to actually perform those tasks.

> **Deliberation is not only the step where the Relentless Search for Better Ways begins, it is a characteristic of how the process works.**

And the process doesn't work without good-faith, active participation by all parties. In this example, the branch managers were effective facilitators. They initiated the process with inquiry, and they sustained it by listening to what the closers had to say and by following up in a timely manner.

The closers quickly came to the realization that the requirements for their success had changed and that sticking with the status quo just wouldn't work. From there it wasn't a question of if they should do something to meet those new requirements. The only question was what they would do. And during the Deliberation step, they provided the answers.

Step 2: Decide

Whew! Did you think we'd never get past deliberation? "We get it, so move on!" is something you may have thought—even uttered—as you plowed through that last section. Hey, deliberation is an important step, and now that we've completed it, let's get on to the next step, one of my personal favorites, "Decide." By the way, one reason deliberation is so important is that it lets you collect the information on which you'll make decisions.

File this away:

> **Deliberation is done in support of, not in lieu of, decision making.**

I'm guessing that most of us have found ourselves in organizations, on committees, or in groups engaged in seemingly endless deliberations: "Let's study this some more." "We'll need to gather some additional information." "Why don't we get input from some more people?" "We simply must have more sampling data." And on and on it goes. For people with an aversion to making decisions, deliberation can provide a safe alternative, the old "we need more information" approach.

The purpose of deliberation in my model is to obtain or develop information that will help us make good decisions, better ones than we might have made without that information. Notice I didn't say anything about them being perfect. If the deliberation was done to identify areas needing improvement, e.g., R&D, production, marketing, sales, then the information obtained or developed during deliberations can help us *decide* which area(s) we'll work on. If we deliberated to identify alternatives to what we're currently doing in one of those areas, e.g., the marketing tools and techniques we're employing, the information we obtained or developed in deliberation will help us *decide* on the alternatives we'll implement.

So it's decision-making time, and the first question is, "Who'll be making those decisions?" Or, as my fourteen-year-old daughter would ask, "Like, who gets to pick?"

Back to your decisions. As I see it, there are a couple of broad options regarding who makes the decisions. Either the facilitator—the person who extended invitations to the deliberations and moderated—or the participants decide. Here are some thoughts on designating decision makers.

No Surprises!

When extending invitations to prospective participants, facilitators should let them know the purpose of the deliberation, including *who will be making decisions* about how to use the information participants provide. If people show up believing they will be making decisions or casting votes for how to proceed beyond the deliberations, they may be unpleasantly surprised to discover that someone else will be making those decisions. Unpleasantly surprised folks will probably share their unhappiness with other potential participants.

**Let people know up front
what you're asking them to contribute
and who will be making decisions about next steps.**

Facilitators Decide (Choose)

We can agree—can't we?—that expanding participation in the Relentless Search for Better Ways is a good idea. Having said that, can we also agree that there will be many situations in which the most qualified person to make post-deliberation decisions is the facilitator? This is especially true in the early stages of utilizing my model. If you're that facilitator and you find yourself in such a situation, don't be timid or apologetic about declaring your intention to make the decision and then stepping up and doing so. In such situations. you're acknowledging the value of participants' perspectives and input, and you're also demonstrating your ultimate accountability for the decision and its consequences.

Participants Decide (Bless)

There will be other situations in which you are confident that participants are able and willing to make decisions. In those cases, delegating decision-making authority makes sense. In addition to freeing you to focus on other matters that require your attention, delegating decision-making authority reinforces your confidence in those whose participation is essential to the plan's success. As they see you expanding their roles, they become more committed to the search. They will provide higher-value input, and they will serve as positive role models for other potential participants.

> **Delegate decision-making authority judiciously and aggressively.**

No, those two characteristics are not mutually exclusive. Look aggressively for opportunities to delegate decision-making authority. After you're confident that the candidates you've selected are ready—*and not before you're confident that they are ready*—tell them to make the decision and let you know what they've decided.

The second step in our search, Decide, begins with shared understanding of who will make decisions about how to proceed, using the information developed during deliberations. For our purposes, we've looked at two types of decisions. The first is determining which area(s) to focus on in our Relentless Search for Better Ways, and the second is selecting the new processes or techniques we'll try.

After these decisions have been made, there are two more things we must do before moving to the third step, Implement. In fact, without the benefit of these next two activities, efforts to implement will prove ineffective. Actually, *unless* we complete these two activities, there probably won't be much in the way of implementation. Before moving to the Implement step, we'll need to define success and create a plan for achieving it.

Define Success

"Ready! FIRE! Aim!" Sound familiar to any of you? It certainly describes the process I've often seen in "rolling out" or "launching" organizational initiatives. Somebody—usually someone hunkered down in an executive office—comes up with a "great idea" for an initiative, which is then handed off to a next-level-down "facilitator." From there, it can take any number of turns, but conspicuously absent from most of the processes I've seen are any rational definitions of success or workable plans.

Back to the areas you've chosen to address or the alternative practices you've decided to implement. There must have been some rationale for selecting those options. There had to be some anticipated, measurable improvements that justified your choosing them, right? Before trying to implement the options selected, let's determine the criteria we'll use to measure progress and to assess the return we're getting on our efforts.

> **We need some way of verifying
> that the alternatives we've chosen
> will yield the value necessary
> to justify our efforts to implement them.**

In some instances, we've made our decisions based on assumptions. Let's be sure to set up ways of testing those assumptions as early as possible in the implementation step.

Likewise, we must establish benchmarks (measures) and timeframes for assessing the effectiveness of our implementation processes. Don't interpret this to mean that you won't have to adjust your measures or timeframes, because you probably will. What I'm saying is that, unless you establish reasonable *definitions* of success or progress and *measures* for assessing your implementation, you may end up pulling the plug on your efforts prematurely. Or, you may persist too long with activities that are taking you nowhere. Without specific, worthwhile, and realistic objectives and measures for providing evidence of progress or success, it'll be mighty difficult to know if what you're trying is a better way—or just different. I try to stay away from change for the sake of change, so I strongly encourage you to define success as part of your pre-implementation process. Lord deliver us from the "change gurus" who go around assuring us that "all change is good." 'Tain't true; some changes are downright bad.

Create Actionable Plans

I know what you're thinking: "If Bearden spends as much time here as he did on deliberation, his treatment of planning will rival *War and Peace*." Take a couple of deep breaths and lighten up. My approach to planning probably isn't what you're expecting.

Do I believe planning is important? Absolutely. Things almost always work out better if you have a plan than if you just wing it. But here's another thought about planning:

> **Planning can be—and often is—overdone.**

That's right, you read it here. There is such a thing as too much planning, and there are among us "professional planners." No, I'm not referring to legitimate professional planners, people who plan events such as weddings—talk about your high-stress jobs. I'm talking instead about people whose primary responsibilities have to do with operations, but who have little time for that because they're too busy planning.

Here's a classic example. Have you ever encountered people who use some form of to-do lists? Have you ever noticed that some of them spend obscene amounts of time developing their to-do lists or filling in the day planners they received when they attended two-day "time management" retreats? Not only do they devote a lot of time to their lists, they seem addicted to the priorities they've assigned the tasks on their lists. If an unexpected event requires their attention, their first response is to check their lists! I'm sorry, but "time management" is one of the great mysteries of life to me. Forgive my diversion and ranting. Now, back to my approach to planning.

We'll usually achieve better results on initiatives if we have plans, right? We've agreed on that point. But no matter how much time and energy we invest in creating plans, what do we discover as soon as we begin implementing them? They all have flaws. We'll encounter unexpected—and, therefore, unplanned for—circumstances. What that means is we'll have to adjust our plans. Activities that we'd expected to yield positive results may not, so our plans must be modified. It's maddening, but true.

The plans you create should be a framework for getting started on the next step in your search, Implementation. Getting started means transitioning from theory (the plan) to practice (implementation). If your plan doesn't provide clear, easily understood, and implementable *initial* steps, there's a good chance that your initiative will languish in the shadowy realm that is "not planning" and "not implementing." Let's all observe a moment of silence for plans relegated to "the graveyard of failed initiatives."

> **Good ideas don't always translate
> into effective action,
> and one reason is that some plans don't include
> specific guidelines for the initial phases of
> implementation.**

Your plans simply must provide clarity on roles and timeframes for implementation. Remember, all the people who participated in your deliberations and all the people whose efforts are needed to implement the plans are busy. Most of them aren't sitting around waiting for assignments. So, when seeking their participation in implementing those plans, you'd better provide them with specific guidance.

Before moving to implementation, we've got to have a plan. It needn't be one that rivals the plan for invading Normandy, just a simple, easily understood set of specific guidelines for getting started. I've come up with a test for determining whether what you've got is a plan or just another idea—maybe even a good idea—that will never go anywhere.

If you can answer the following question, you've got yourself a plan:

> Who'll do what by when?

If you and the other participants *do not* have the same answers to that question, your first priority is to make sure you do. Without that information, your implementation efforts will be short-lived, at best. If you and the other participants *do* have the same answers to that question, you're ready to move to the next step in the search, Implement.

Step 3: Implement

"Implement" is to "plan" as "fire" is to "aim." You can aim at a target, maintaining a perfect sight picture, but unless you pull the trigger (fire), you'll make no impact on the target. Likewise, unless you implement them, your plans will do nothing to move you closer to your objectives.

We can go further with this analogy. Even after taking careful aim and firing, you still might miss your target. Just because you aimed and fired, you aren't guaranteed a hit. Same with plans and their implementation. No guarantees. But just as aiming carefully and firing will get you closer to your target than just "shooting from the hip," having a plan and then implementing it will produce better results than "making it up as you go."

My key point here is that plans are not worth much until and unless they are implemented. To produce results, ideas must be translated into action.

Here's a brief chronology of how we got to this step, Implement:

1. Deliberate: Facilitators and participants identified and assigned priorities to options for consideration in the Relentless Search for Better Ways. Those options include areas in

which improvements are needed and/or alternative processes or practices.

2. Decide: Options were selected, criteria and measures for assessing progress were established, and plans were developed. Participants and facilitators left this step agreeing on who would do what by when.

Guess what. It's "when"—the time for "who" to do "what"—and we call that step
Implement. Since the term and concept are self-explanatory, I won't belabor either. Instead, I'll focus on behaviors that can delay or devalue implementation. I'll conclude with some thoughts about a popular buzzword, "team player."

Confusion About Decisions

No, I don't mean that people don't understand the decisions. OK, sometimes that can be the case, and if it is, you'll need to address their misunderstanding. If people have legitimate questions about which decisions have been made, then by all means, explain those decisions to them. Explanations should include the three components we covered way back in deliberations, "whats," "whys," and "hows":

1. Tell them *what* was decided, e.g., the areas to be addressed and/or the alternative practices to be implemented.

2. Explain the rationale for the decisions, e.g., *why* those areas were chosen and/or why the alternative practices will be implemented.

3. Finally, describe the overall scope of implementation, who'll do what, by when.

When I cite "confusion" as a behavior that delays implementation, I am referring to the apparent confusion some people exhibit about how they should respond to the decisions.

> **Some people seem to think that decisions are invitations to do more deliberation.**

Those people must understand that, after the decisions are made and the plans developed and announced, the time for deliberation is over—for now.

Some of you have had first-hand experience using some variation of my Relentless Search for Better Ways Model. Many of you have invited staff members to participate in the decision-making process by brainstorming areas to improve and/or ways to make improvements in those areas. What you've no doubt found is that some people resist, or even reject, your invitations to participate in the deliberative process. They're "too busy," they "don't care," or they see such activities as "somebody else's job." Whatever their reasons, they opt out of the deliberations—temporarily.

They are unwilling to deliberate when asked to do so, but when decisions are made without their input, they exhibit confusion about appropriate next steps. Some of these people seem to think that decisions are the *real* invitations to deliberate. All you have to do to raise their interest in sharing their thoughts is announce decisions that require something from them. Suddenly they have the time and interest that were in such short supply before. They are ready—at last—to deliberate. But for now, that step is complete.

Let's go back to the Bearden home for a classic example of this "confusion" about what decisions are. Not surprisingly, this classic example was a situation involving the young man who has single-handedly provided much of my anecdotal material, the one and only Ryan Matthew Bearden. You'll remember him from his lead role in the night of "three boys, some beer, and a cop."

When Ryan was twelve years old or so, Barbara and I decided to put together a "job description" (list of chores) and "comp plan" (allowance) for the lad. Being quite progressive, we decided to include Ryan in our decision-making process. That may not sound all that progressive to some of you, but allow me to contrast our approach to how my Dad made a similar decision when I was twelve. When I allowed as how I needed more money, his response was exactly what you'd expect from a guy who survived the Depression and went off to France and Germany to save the world: "Get a job." Back to progressive Barb and Jim.

We extended an invitation to young Ryan, thinking that he would leap at the opportunity to participate in deliberations on topics so important to him, his labor and his money. To our surprise, Ryan rejected our invitation. Being a twelve-year-old boy, his social calendar was simply too full to allow his participation, so he graciously suggested that Barb and I make the decision and let him know what it was. And that's what we did.

Do I have to tell you how Ryan responded when we announced our decision, listing the chores he would perform and how he would be compensated? Suddenly he couldn't wait to deliberate. He had plenty of ideas about the chores, the comp, and—I suspect—the prospect of having to live with two idiots.

And our response? Been there, done that (deliberation), and now it's time for the next step, Implement. We assured him that we would gladly sit down with him and revisit our decision *in six months*, and then suggested that what he needed to do was start the lawn mower. Note: One of the reasons we can't wait to have grandchildren is that we are so eager to see our children assume our roles, while we function as their children's advocates.

When people disagree with decisions, they can air their differences with the person(s) who made the decisions, or with others. Both of these options represent attempts to replace Implement with Deliberate. While we appreciate their interest—albeit untimely interest—in deliberation, we will not delay implementing the plans we've developed in order to accommodate their untimely arrival "at the table."

Team Players

Again, when you get to this third step, Implement, the time for deliberation is over—for now. It is time to set aside whatever differences you may have with the decisions and do your part to implement them. In short, it's time to behave like a "team player." The distinction between team members and team players is nothing more than their different levels of commitment and participation in crucial organizational processes. As buzzwords go, "team player" sure seems to be one of the all-time favorites. It seems that, at every turn, we are encouraged to be team players. Such encouragement usually comes from people who want us to go along with them or the policies they're charged with enforcing. It's a desperate, often whiny, plea, "Come on, be a team player." Since it's used so much, there can be some confusion about just what it means.

This third step in the Relentless Search for Better Ways, Implement, provides an opportunity to see team players in action, to identify one of their defining characteristics.

> **Team Players are willing to temporarily set aside their individual agendas in deference to supporting their teams' agendas.**

As a result of the deliberative process, decisions will be made. Regardless of what those decisions are, there will be people who disagree with them. In some instances, those people will have voiced their opinions during the deliberations, only to have the decisions go counter to what they had suggested. When that happens, those people have options, and the option they choose will reveal which of them are real team players.

One option available to them is to air their objections. They can air their objections with the person(s) who made the decisions, and I refer to that as an appropriate forum. Appropriate forums are ones that include—may be limited to—the person(s) who can do something about the objections. If someone is unhappy with a decision, the appropriate person to speak with is the person who made the decision.

Other forums are, in most instances, inappropriate. Inappropriate forums are ones that include people who did not make the decisions, but whose efforts are needed for their implementation. If these people did not make the decision, then they are probably not in positions to change it. They may not even be able to explain the decision, at least not as well as the person who made it.

Whether it's in appropriate or inappropriate forums, airing differences after decisions are made and announced does little to support implementation.

The other option available to people who disagree with decisions is to temporarily set aside their differences and put a good-faith effort into implementing those decisions. Clearly, the people who exercise this option are the ones I would view as true team players.

The only way plans produce value is if they are implemented. It is through implementation that progress is made. Only through implementation will you discover the flaws in your plans.

The flaws are the focus of the fourth step in the search, Improve. Making continuous improvements is very important since it's the only reason to embark on this Relentless Search for Better Ways. The next chapter is devoted exclusively to this all-important step in the search.

Chapter 6 Summary

The Relentless Search for Better Ways
A Model for Collaborative Processes

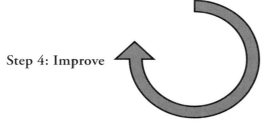

- When inviting people to participate in Step 1, Deliberate, you'll improve the quality of their input by giving them advance notice—time to think.

- You initiate deliberation by asking questions. You sustain it by listening to participants' responses to your questions.

- The information you ask participants to share should include: whats, whys and hows.

- Deliberation is done in support of—not in lieu of—decision-making.

- Determine and announce in advance who will be making decisions using the information obtained in deliberation.

- Delegate decision-making authority judiciously and aggressively. Those 2 characteristics are not mutually exclusive.

- Establish criteria and methodologies for verifying that the alternatives you've chosen to implement are really better ways, and not just different.

- Good plans must include specific guidelines for the initial phases of implementation.

- If you know who'll do what by when, you've got yourself a plan.

- Unless they are effectively implemented, your plans will do nothing to move you closer to achieving your objectives.

- Some people seem to think that decisions are nothing more than invitations to do more deliberation. Those people are mistaken.

- After decisions are made, the time for deliberation about those decisions is over.

- When you get to the third step, Implement, it is time for all parties to set aside their differences with the decision and put good-faith effort into implementing it.

- Team players are willing to temporarily set aside their individual agendas in deference to supporting their teams' agendas.

Chapter 7

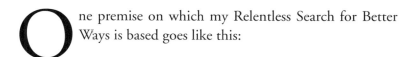

Continuous Process Improvement

One premise on which my Relentless Search for Better Ways is based goes like this:

> **If we haven't found a better way,
> it's only because we haven't looked.**

You'll recall my offering that premise as a modified version of the often used, but highly questionable alternative: "If it ain't broke, don't fix it."

So we've embarked on our Relentless Search for Better Ways. We've deliberated, decided, and are now engaged in implementing the changes we've selected. Just because we're performing alternative tasks or employing different techniques, don't think our Relentless Search for Better Ways is over. We'll need to periodically step back from our implementation efforts and identify ways to improve on what we're doing. Are we relentless, or what?

Step 4: Improve

The Improve step is a return to deliberation. In this step, we'll evaluate the actions we've taken and the results those actions have produced. We'll look at the processes we've employed in implementation and the outcomes or progress those processes have yielded. Not surprisingly, I've got some suggestions for how to break the processes down.

It's important that you identify every opportunity to improve, while still acknowledging the progress that *has* been made and the people who have contributed to making that progress. In fact, that's where I suggest you begin, by acknowledging the activities and people producing favorable results.

What's Working

In order to sustain the Relentless Search for Better Ways, facilitators must continue to facilitate and encourage team members' participation at every step. In order to sustain team members' participation, facilitators must retain their own credibility. Few things undermine a facilitator's credibility more than failure to recognize and acknowledge progress.

How many of you have worked for bosses, played for coaches, played instruments for directors, or studied under teachers who focused only on your mistakes? I suspect we all have, and I'm guessing that, after a while, we came to suspect the credibility of those "mentors." No matter how inept we might have been, there were times when our performance showed at least hints of improvement. *We* noticed, so why didn't they? Their failure to acknowledge our progress, no matter how slight, probably led us to conclude that those instructors, coaches, directors or bosses either didn't notice or didn't care enough about us to say anything even remotely positive. Based on those conclusions, how eager were we to continue working on the skills they were purportedly trying to help us learn? Some people are so driven to learn, so grateful for access to "master" teachers, or so happy to have jobs that they'll endure this singular focus on their faults. But most people will not.

> **If you want people to participate actively
> in the search for better ways,
> with its inevitable setbacks and mistakes,
> you'd better do more than just
> point out their mistakes.**

As facilitators of the search, you must pay attention to the people working to implement those "better ways." Since the things they're doing may be totally new to them, there will be plenty of mistakes. If you pay close attention, however, you'll also detect signs of progress in the quality of their efforts and the results their efforts produce. Look for evidence of progress, and when you find it, acknowledge it. Let the people who're working to implement those "better ways" know that you are aware of, and appreciate, their efforts.

In some instances, mistakes or setbacks will actually be the first signs of progress. When people get up the gumption to try something new, they will make mistakes, especially early on. Use those early mistakes to acknowledge and praise their courage for stepping up and trying new things.

When you begin by acknowledging progress and individual contributions, you're letting people know that you are paying attention, not just to their mistakes, but also to their successes. You will earn and retain credibility as a facilitator. Then, they'll respond favorably when you do point out their mistakes.

One closing thought about acknowledging people's successes: *Don't make them up!* Credibility is a powerful, but fragile, thing. Don't jeopardize yours by fabricating examples of progress. If you pay close enough attention, you won't have to.

> **Successes, or signs of progress,
> don't have to be earth-shattering,
> but they do have to be legitimate.**

What's Not Working

When you're engaged in the Relentless Search for Better Ways and playing to win, setbacks are inevitable. Here's a reminder:

> **Setbacks will almost always have impacts on us,
> but the choices we make *about* those setbacks
> are often more powerful, have more impact,
> than the setbacks themselves.**

I've made that point a couple of times already, so you should know how important I believe choices are. Let me take a moment here to use the experiences of a well-known sports figure to reinforce my point about the power of our choices in the face of setbacks.

Actually, all I need to do here is mention that person's name. It's Lance Armstrong. Need I say more? In the midst of training toward the goal of becoming one of the world's premier bicyclists, this man encountered a setback of mighty proportions. The diagnosis was cancer, and the prognosis was guarded, at best. To combat the disease, Armstrong had to undergo treatment that would batter his body and wreak havoc with his training. But what was the outcome?

Not only did he win his battle with cancer and return to his sport, Armstrong established a new standard of excellence, winning an unprecedented seven consecutive Tour de France victories. We would all acknowledge the importance of medical intervention, and many would also acknowledge the power of divine intervention. However, we all surely would agree that before either of those forms of intervention could get traction, Armstrong had to make some choices. Key among them: he had to choose how he would respond to the diagnosis. Would he throw in the towel, or would he fight? It sure seems to me that he chose the latter.

We don't get to choose the hands we're dealt, but we always make choices about them. Lance Armstrong's victory over cancer sure illustrates for me the power of the choices we make about the inevitable setbacks we'll encounter.

Back to our Relentless Search for Better Ways and the choices we make about setbacks. Some of the "victim" choices we discussed earlier were denying, blaming, wallowing, quitting, waiting, wishing, and hoping. How's that for a lineup? When such choices are made, the search for better ways grinds to a halt.

Facilitating the Search

Facilitators play a key role in influencing the type of choices made about setbacks. Are you starting to get the impression that facilitators are pretty important to sustaining our search? I hope so.

In the wake of setbacks, facilitators have opportunities to achieve several key objectives. Doing so will not only sustain team members in their search roles, it will also help the facilitators identify and develop the next generation of facilitators.

> After acknowledging the positives,
> facilitators must ensure
> that all parties recognize what's not working,
> the parts of the plan that must be improved.

This can be done by pointing out setbacks and mistakes, or by asking others for their observations. As you might suspect, I favor the latter approach, since it gives the people who've had firsthand experience with the setbacks the opportunity to point them out. Those engaged in implementation can often detect weaknesses in plans that facilitators might miss.

Remember, one of the things I encouraged you to do in Step 2, Decide, was to define success. That included establishing criteria, timeframes, and processes for assessing progress. Completing that step will help you and your team evaluate your plans and implementation efforts.

Find the Lessons in the Mistakes

The only way to improve the parts of your plan or implementation processes that aren't working is to identify alternatives that might. That's the approach I encourage facilitators to take in this phase of the search for better ways.

> **After identifying the parts of the plan and implementation that are not working, facilitators should shift the team's focus off the flaws, mistakes or setbacks and begin looking for possible alternatives (better ways).**

Facilitating the shift from mistakes to lessons is an extremely important and potentially powerful example of leadership. Facilitators who effectively do so reinforce the confidence they've expressed in team members and in their ability to participate in all phases of the search. They also enhance team members' comfort with the process by demonstrating that they will focus more of their attention on the lessons and less on the mistakes. Facilitators (leaders) who do this increase team members' willingness to participate actively in the Relentless Search for Better Ways by creating and sustaining cultures that are Change-Friendly.

> **Identifying the lessons to be learned from mistakes made in planning and/or implementation is best accomplished as a team exercise, and not unilaterally by facilitators.**

Here's what facilitators have done so far in Step 4, Improve:

1. Acknowledged progress and team members' contributions.
2. Facilitated analysis of plans and their implementation, including:
   - What's not working: the flaws, mistakes or setbacks.

- Alternatives to what's not working: the next generation of "better ways."

The next steps are really just variations on Step 2, Decide, and Step 3, Implement. After identifying possible alternatives to what's not working, either the facilitators or team members must select the new alternatives they'll try. For the options chosen, they must then define success and develop plans. The obvious next step is to implement the modified plan and, at some predetermined time, step back and do some more improving.

So, as you can see, this model really is a cycle, an ongoing effort to improve on processes and produce ever-improving results. To sustain participants' comfort with the search, facilitators can make and keep a commitment with them, and the Improve step is the ideal place to do so.

After dissecting and analyzing plans and their implementation, identifying mistakes, and choosing new, alternative activities and techniques, facilitators should reinforce their commitment to finding better ways—not to finding fault.

Remember, Apply and Forget

Most of us have heard it said that if we don't remember our mistakes we're destined to repeat them. I don't believe that in the literal sense. It seems to me that remembering mistakes can actually be a recipe for repeating them. If you hit a bad golf or tennis shot, do you try to recall that mistake when you hit your next shot? If so, if you replay that mistake in your mind, you actually increase the likelihood of repeating it.

One reason even professional golf and tennis players use coaches is to help them learn from—and not remember—their mistakes. One of the things good coaches try to do is correct the mistakes that produce bad shots. After learning correct technique, what value is there in recalling mistakes? Mental imagery has long been used by top performers in many fields. You can be sure that the images they hold in mind are not the mistakes they've made, but the correct techniques they've learned. Those would be the lessons.

If we don't *learn* anything from our mistakes, and if we don't remember and apply those lessons, we stand a good chance of repeating the mistakes.

> As facilitators, you must encourage people to remember and apply the lessons *and forget the mistakes.*

You can reinforce that commitment by not reminding people of mistakes after the lessons have been extracted from those experiences.

As with most suggestions, this one has a caveat. When people demonstrate an inability or unwillingness to learn from their mistakes, they create situations that must be confronted. Repeating the same mistakes, or variations of those mistakes, indicates an inability or unwillingness to learn. (More about that in Chapter 8.)

Most people, when given legitimate reasons and ample opportunities to do so, will make good-faith efforts to participate in the search for better ways. As with most other initiatives, the search may get "old" (the "new" wears off) before its full benefits are realized. Without effective facilitation, the search can become just another failed initiative, an all-too-common organizational phenomenon.

"Initiative du Jour"

Does that have a familiar ring? Many companies have long histories of ideas that became initiatives, and initiatives that went, well, nowhere. Died on the vine.

It doesn't take too many of these before the staff becomes accustomed to—even expects—much talk and little action. The "rollout" of each new initiative is greeted with a collective rolling of eyes and rumors that if "we just lay low, this one will blow over so we can get back to the way we've always done things."

An interesting point about these initiatives is that many of them made sense. No one could argue with the need, shortcoming, or opportunity that they were designed to address. But logic just wasn't enough.

My guess is that this is a widespread malady. I would further surmise that organizational and individual progress would improve dramatically if those initiatives got enough traction to produce some initial results. That traction would create the momentum necessary for the initiatives to really pay off, in at least two ways.

First, the ultimate payoff is that they would address the problems or opportunities for which they were developed and would generate some economic value.

Secondly—and, in some cases, more importantly—these successes would reinforce the efforts of their proponents and give cynics cause to rethink their cynicism.

> **Initiatives that produce results can help convert a culture from change-averse to change-friendly.**

Culture and the Search

It is difficult to overstate the importance of culture. Out in the real world, corporate culture trumps initiatives. No matter how much sense an initiative makes, no matter how logical it seems; the organizational culture, not the logic, will determine the initiative's fate.

> **"Bad" cultures eat "good" initiatives alive.**

In Chapter 4, I extolled the virtues of change-friendly cultures. Unfortunately, such cultures are exceptions. Without a change-friendly culture, the quality of plans or initiatives suffers, and implementation is often ineffective.

A few years ago, a client asked me to share with him the one distinguishing characteristic I'd seen in successful people and organizations. Without hesitation, I gave him the same answer I would give him today:

> **Successful people and organizations demonstrate a willingness to consider and try alternatives to the status quo.**

Actually, they're more than just willing, they're eager to do so. Successful people are actively engaged in the Relentless Search for Better Ways. *When those people find themselves in leadership positions, they facilitate expanded participation in that search.*

One might think that developing and launching initiatives is a good example of someone engaged in this relentless search. If the initiatives produced results, then I would agree. But when they don't, when they repeatedly go nowhere, then the search hasn't really begun.

Back to the "initiative du jour." We've seen that many of them are based on sound logic, at least regarding the areas they're designed to address. But since they're stillborn, the Relentless Search for Better Ways must extend beyond their potential value and focus on two key stages in their life cycles: their design and their implementation.

Initiative Design

Leaders *must* function effectively as facilitators. Even in small companies, presidents, CEOs, or other leaders simply cannot perform all the tasks necessary for organizational success. A leader's success is ultimately determined by the choices that other people make and the consequences those choices produce. Same with initiatives. In order for them to get traction, gain momentum, and produce their intended results, other people must get actively involved.

> **One reason so many initiatives fall flat is because leaders don't get key people involved in the *design* phase.**

When I say "key people," I'm talking about the people whose efforts will be required for the implementation and ultimate success of those initiatives.

Back to logic. We've agreed that many failed initiatives have good logic behind them. The leader who recognizes an area in need of addressing—a problem, potential problem, or an untapped opportunity—can use logic as the basis for calling together a group of people with the perspective, skills, and experience to figure out how to address it. I call that deliberation.

Those people may have little or no experience in actually designing initiatives. Remember, in most organizations, initiatives have been created and handed down. What that means is their initial designs and plans will most certainly have flaws. But by having key people design the initiatives, and by making it clear that designs and plans are not expected to be perfect, leaders create cultures that support trial and error. And that sure seems to make sense to me, since almost every worthwhile improvement ever made included healthy doses of trial and error.

Which would you prefer, an initiative that goes nowhere because no one gets behind it, or one that moves slowly at first because it must be fine-tuned? With the first option, you have no progress. With the second, you have slow initial progress, but eventual results.

Follow-Up

"What gets measured, gets done." I'm sure you've heard that. Based on my experience, it's the truth. Here's another way of saying it:

> A missing ingredient in many failed initiatives is any meaningful follow-up or oversight by people in leadership positions.

In most organizations, the leaders, or more accurately, people in leadership positions, will hunker down in their offices and hammer out new and exciting initiatives, which they then hand over to the people they expect to implement them. Those people already have plenty to do, so when a new initiative is laid on them, their first question is likely to be, "Just how important is this one?" If they ask that question, they'll receive verbal assurance that this one is very important to the people "at the top."

But when there is no follow-up from those "top" people, the message is clear. If there is disparity between what gets said and what gets done, the behavior—or lack thereof—carries the day.

Where failed initiatives are concerned, the Relentless Search for Better Ways must include—begin with—the role leaders have played in the design and implementation of those initiatives. Too often, those leaders are far too involved in their design and far too uninvolved in their implementation. And this brings me to our next topic: the role of leaders in the Relentless Search for Better Ways.

Chapter 7 Summary

- In the 4th step in the Relentless Search for Better Ways, Improve, we look at the implementation process and the results that process has produced.

- As a facilitator, look for evidence of progress, and when you find it, acknowledge it.

- Success or signs of progress don't have to be earth shattering, but they do have to be legitimate. Don't make them up.

- After acknowledging the positives, facilitators must ensure that all parties recognize what's not working, the parts of the plan that must be improved.

- After identifying the parts of the plan and implementation that are not working, facilitators should shift the team's focus off the flaws, mistakes or setbacks and begin looking for possible alternatives (better ways).

- As facilitators you must encourage people to remember and apply the lessons and forget the mistakes.

- "Bad" cultures eat "good" initiatives alive.

- One reason so many initiatives fall flat is because leaders don't get key people involved in the *design* phase.

- A missing ingredient in most failed initiatives is any meaningful follow-up or oversight by people in leadership positions.

Chapter 8

Leadership

What do you think the chances are that I can adequately cover the topic of leadership in one chapter? If you said, "Slim to none," you were right, so I'm not even going to try. What I will do is share some thoughts about the crucial roles leaders play in the Relentless Search for Better Ways. Contrary to what you may have concluded after counterproductive encounters with "pretenders" at leadership, effective leadership is a prerequisite for sustained organizational success.

By "pretenders," I'm referring to people who may occupy leadership positions but who don't really provide effective leadership. These people may have titles, authority, and offices with windows, but when it comes to actually leading, they can only "pretend." I'm guessing you've encountered one or more of them. The roles leaders play will determine whether or not the search ever begins, and if it does, whether or not it is sustained long enough to actually produce results.

Roles Leaders Play

Let's do a quick exercise to help define what leaders do—or what people expect them to do. What would you list as the single most important task leaders perform? As with other questions we've pondered, there are plenty of possible responses, so you'll just have to settle for mine at the moment. As I see it:

> **Effective leaders facilitate crucial organizational processes**

There is a big difference between being a facilitator and being a *doer*. This is an important distinction for us to consider. People are often promoted into leadership positions because of their success as doers. They performed their assigned tasks better than their peers, and their performance paid off in promotions. Not surprisingly, many of those "rookie leaders" don't make the transition from doers (people who perform specific operational tasks), to facilitators (people who influence others to higher levels of performance). They may *occupy* leadership positions, but they do not provide effective leadership.

Here's an almost paradoxical leadership concept:

> **As facilitators,
> leaders directly impact crucial organizational processes
> by addressing them indirectly.**

This is a subtle, but extremely important, point about leadership and facilitation. We can readily see its application to leaders' roles in creating organizational cultures. Leaders drive cultures, not by holding meetings or rallies to discuss or promote the culture, but by modeling the behavior they expect from others. Their behaviors "trickle down" to create the overall culture.

The influence of culture on the choices people operating in that culture make cannot be overstated. If the organization's culture is change-friendly, then people in that organization will be encouraged to participate actively in the Relentless Search for Better Ways. Leaders create such a culture by their behavior.

Sales management provides another good example of this phenomenon. Sales managers directly impact sales results not by making all the sales calls themselves, but by influencing the choices that salespeople make. That influence can take a variety of forms. Managers can demonstrate sales techniques while accompanying salespeople on calls. They can reinforce the importance of preferred activities by tracking salespeople's performance of those activities. Their behavior is a powerful influencer of the choices the salespeople make. Leaders in a sales division directly impact sales results by addressing them indirectly—by facilitating crucial phases of the sales process.

Facilitation and Initiatives

The Relentless Search for Better Ways is a process for identifying viable alternatives to the status quo. Those alternatives often take the form of initiatives. In Chapters 5, 6, and 7, we worked through the collaborative process by which initiatives are designed, executed, and fine-tuned.

But not all initiatives originate with the people responsible for their execution. Some are handed down from "on high." Often the brainchildren of strategic leaders (executives), most of these handed-down initiatives contain some potential for producing benefits. But before they can do so, they must be executed, and that's where facilitation is so important.

I refer to the people responsible for facilitating timely, effective execution of these initiatives as "leaders at the points of contact." Here's another thought about the importance of leaders functioning effectively as facilitators:

In order to produce benefits, initiatives must be executed. Without effective facilitation, execution won't happen.

Let's look at four key steps for facilitating execution:

1. Understanding expectations.
2. Moving from strategies to tactics.
3. Developing actionable plans.
4. Doing timely, aggressive follow-up.

Understanding Expectations

Initiatives created by strategic leaders almost always contain language about the initiatives' goals. Not surprisingly, the language used to describe these strategic expectations is often quite broad. For example, a client for whom I've recently done some work is merging two operational units. Two of the expectations that came down "from on high" to the tactical leaders were "to form a common culture" and "teamwork."

Surely no one could quarrel with the value of a common, healthy culture or of functioning as a team, but would you agree that the stated goals leave a lot of room for interpretation? Before any meaningful, sustained execution can occur, these strategic expectations must be translated into specific activities. Next, employees at the operational levels must perform those activities.

Step back for a minute and think about some of the initiatives that have been rolled out in your organizations. Would you agree that many of them come to the operational levels with only broad definitions of what is expected? Others may be better defined, but even for those, there are probably few specific directions or suggestions for how the expectations will be met.

Reflecting back on my experiences with organizational clients, here are two more examples of broad expectations:

1. "Exceed expectations."
2. "Improve relationships between departments."

From Strategic to Tactical

Those strategic expectations may express their originators' vision, but what's missing? We have a pretty good idea of what the initiatives are designed to produce, but we're provided very little in the way of guidance for how to proceed. The absence of clarity about how to implement initiatives dooms many of them to quick deaths. So, obtaining that essential clarity is the first step in facilitating execution.

> **Translating strategic expectations into specific activities for people at the operational levels is a crucial first step in facilitating execution.**

Who better to do that than *leaders* at the operational levels? Strategies are swell, but without supporting tactics, strategies just won't fly. Leaders at the points of contact facilitate execution by translating broad—maybe even vague—objectives into specific, actionable plans.

If strategic expectations are too vague, tactical leaders must obtain clarity from "up the chain." For example, what does "exceed expectations" mean, in measurable terms? When they're encouraged to "improve relationships between departments," what exactly does that mean? What criteria will be used to track progress? What do "improved relationships" look like? Before tactical leaders can facilitate the creation of actionable plans, they must be clear on the goals.

Develop Actionable Plans

After identifying the specific objectives the initiatives have been developed to achieve, tactical leaders move to the third step in facilitation. Here, they begin formulating plans for achieving those objectives.

> **Actionable plans must include specific *activities*
> to be performed by specific *people*
> within specific *timeframes*.**

What you're looking for here are answers to the question I raised in Chapter 6: "Who'll do what, by when?" Developing such plans can be done by leaders alone or collaboratively. There are pros and cons associated with each approach.

Unilateral vs. Collaborative Planning

The obvious advantage of the unilateral approach is the speed with which plans can be created. When only one person's ideas are in play, there's no time required to reach consensus, consider different positions, or answer questions. If getting going quickly is your top consideration, the unilateral approach is the way to go. But when developing plans that require buy-in by other people—that would be most plans, now wouldn't it?—the one-person approach leaves a lot to be desired. A whole lot!

Just like initiatives that are developed and then "lobbed" to the people who will implement them, the unilateral approach to planning will often produce plans with serious deficiencies, no matter how quickly they were cranked out. Ironically, plans that are produced unilaterally may require less time on the front end, but whatever time is saved in developing such plans will almost always be lost during their implementation. In fact, the time required to correct later problems will probably be greater than the time saved in planning. Add to that the time required to "sell" those plans to their ultimate implementers, and it becomes evident that unilateral planning really isn't a more expeditious approach.

> **I strongly encourage tactical leaders to employ a collaborative approach for translating strategic expectations into actionable plans.**

Identify the people who will play key roles in implementing the plans and include them in the planning process. Their participation will improve the plan and will help secure their commitment to its proper execution.

So you've got yourself a plan, and it's being executed. Time to kick back and wait for the results to start pouring in, right? Are you kidding? You have completed the first phase by developing a plan—collaboratively, I hope—but successful execution requires a sustained commitment to process improvement. Remember, we've committed to a Relentless Search for Better Ways.

So if anything, effective tactical leadership becomes even more important once the plan is developed and being executed.

Newly developed plans can generate some excitement. After all, they represent something new. Since there are benefits associated with them, people may be enthusiastic in the early phases of execution. This is especially true for people who have participated in developing the plans. But as we saw in our discussion of the Happily Ever After myth, the "new" will most certainly wear off long before people's efforts produce the results being sought. As the "new" wears off, the initial enthusiasm begins to wane. Unless something happens, the quality of effort will probably decline. Follow-up is the "something" that must happen, and if it doesn't happen, you can put a fork in the initiative; it's "done."

Timely, Aggressive Follow-Up

That brings us to the fourth component of facilitation, follow-up. Just as facilitation is one of the most important roles leaders play, follow-up is one of the most important parts of facilitation. Ironically, it is also the one that is most often neglected—or even abdicated.

Here is a frequently used, accurate observation on the importance of follow-up:

> **What gets measured, gets done.**
> **What doesn't get measured, doesn't get done.**

Leaders whose approach to facilitation is collaborative, who include team members in planning, will probably get *initial* buy-in on the plans created. Their team members may hit the ground running and put forth good effort to implement the plans they helped create.

However, here are a couple of things leaders must keep in mind about plans and early implementation efforts:

1. The "new" will wear off the plans, and their implementation, before many meaningful results are produced. Gratification from measurable results will probably be a longer-term phenomenon.
2. Setbacks are inevitable. No matter how much time and effort you put into formulating plans, parts of them will prove to be ineffective.
3. People generally choose the familiar over the unfamiliar, and the "painless" over the "painful." When the initial enthusiasm for new plans wears off—and it always will—people are left with the unfamiliar (different tasks or techniques) and the "painful" (the setbacks associated with those tasks or techniques).

If you think that sounds like a recipe for folding tents and abandoning the plan before it achieves any traction, momentum, or results, you're absolutely right. Without aggressive, timely follow-up, that's exactly what will happen. So what does follow-up mean, and what does it look like?

What Follow-Up Means

To follow up means to assess the efforts being made to implement a plan, and the progress those efforts are producing. It means being out front, out where implementation and execution are happening, out in the implementers' real worlds. It means demonstrating your interest in, and commitment to, the Relentless Search for Better Ways. It means "inspecting what you expect." This is how leaders facilitate execution.

What Follow-Up Looks Like

Follow-up is what leaders *do*. It marks the difference between leaders who facilitate the performance of doers and people in leadership positions who never get past being doers themselves. Instead of inspiring and mentoring people to higher levels of performance, people in that second group simply perform the tasks themselves.

> **While their styles or approaches will vary, effective leaders facilitate the execution of initiatives and implementation of plans by providing appropriate, timely, and relentless follow-up.**

Follow-up can take a variety of forms, and here are four that come to mind:

1. Celebrate.
2. Console.
3. Coach.
4. Confront.

Celebrate

The feedback leaders obtain through observation and inquiry will call for different responses, and one such response is celebration. No, I'm not saying we should look for every chance to shut down operations and throw a party, but I am suggesting that some form of celebration—when appropriate—can be a powerful leadership tool.

If the plan includes new activities or different techniques for the implementers, you can be sure there will be some apprehension and missteps early on. People may be subconsciously looking for reasons to abandon the new, uncomfortable activities or techniques and return to the old, comfortable status quo. Leaders understand this and, in the early phase of implementation, they look for *any* signs of progress. And when they find these signs, they celebrate with the people they've "caught" doing something well, or maybe even poorly. "What? you say. Why would we celebrate something done poorly? The answer is found in one word in the question: "done."

One reason many people avoid trying new things is their fear of making mistakes, especially mistakes that can be seen by people whose opinions matter to them. Some people are especially reluctant to try new things, and when they do so, it represents a breakthrough for them.

> **When you see people trying something new or different, no matter how poorly they may be performing, celebrate their *effort*.**

Acknowledge and honor the courage and initiative they've displayed, and let them know how much you appreciate them for doing so.

Here are a couple of tips about this important form of follow-up:

1. Celebrate publicly, for others to see and hear. Do this even for people who claim that they don't need public recognition—especially for those people.

2. Don't make it up! The efforts you acknowledge and celebrate don't have to be earth-shattering, but they do have to be legitimate.

Console

By now you know that an increase in setbacks is one indication that the Search for Better Ways is *under* way. While I'm convinced that the choices people make about setbacks are more powerful—ultimately have more impact on them—than the setbacks themselves, the setbacks *do* have impacts on them. Most of us would prefer not to encounter setbacks. When we do, most of us will engage in some form of grieving. Hopefully, our grieving will be appropriate to the situation, or as I put it, "rational." Disappointment falls into the appropriate, rational category; devastation does not.

Consoling people who are expressing appropriate, rational feelings about setbacks is something leaders can do to help them get past those setbacks. It's a means of expediting their transition from "grieving" to learning.

> **One of the things people need is validation of, and empathy for, their grieving. If they don't get it, they may escalate their expressions of grief.**

When leaders offer consolation and express empathy for team members' feelings, they help them get closure on the grieving process and shift their thoughts and feelings to learning from—and moving beyond—the setback. Consolation can also reduce team members' need to engage in grieving that is disproportionate to the setbacks they encounter.

Coach

Leaders can help team members shift from grieving to learning from their mistakes by shifting their role from comforter to coach.

The fourth step in my Relentless Search for Better Ways model in Chapter 6 provides some helpful tips for coaching, so you may want to refer back to it. In the coaching mode, leaders facilitate learning, and most setbacks provide excellent learning opportunities. After empathizing with team members about setbacks, leaders can gently, but firmly, move them toward recovering and/or learning from them. I have found that inquiry—asking and listening—is an effective technique for facilitating this shift.

The questions you'll use will vary, but here are some general types of questions for facilitating the shift from grieving to learning:

1. Ask people who have experienced setbacks to describe the setbacks.
2. Ask them to describe the roles they played.
3. Ask about the things they did that *did* appear to work, the things that were at least semi-effective.
4. Ask them to identify the mistakes they made, the things they did or didn't do that contributed to the setback.
5. Ask them to identify possible alternatives to the things that didn't work; what they would do differently if they had it to do over again; and the lessons they've learned from this setback.
6. Ask them what, if anything, they can do to recover what was lost.

This list illustrates a key point I want to make about coaching. Do not be bashful about having people acknowledge their mistakes. There is no dishonor in making mistakes, especially those made in pursuit of better ways. The dishonor most of us associate with mistakes has its origin in the way people who were important to us—parents, teachers, coaches, clergy, bosses—may have reacted to our mistakes in the past. So make sure that you are relentless in ferreting out mistakes—*but don't stop with the mistakes!* After identifying—or helping others identify—the mistakes made, shift your attention away from the mistakes and toward identifying the lessons "hiding" within the mistakes.

OK, the lessons aren't really hiding. Every setback has lessons for us, but in order to identify and benefit from the lessons, we've got to find them. And in order to find the lessons, we've got to look for them.

> **Learning is one of the crucial processes that leaders facilitate. Setbacks provide excellent opportunities for them to do so.**

Here's an example. Our daughters have played club volleyball for several years, and every year they've had different coaches. The ones who have been the most effective, the ones our daughters have enjoyed playing for the most, have been the ones who got beyond the girls' mistakes. Oh, they have been relentless in pointing out poor techniques, but after doing so, they have been even more relentless in coaching the girls on the correct techniques: the lessons.

When people who look to you for leadership see that you are far more interested in the lessons than in the mistakes, they will be much more comfortable trying new activities, and they'll be far more willing to acknowledge their mistakes. The sooner they make and acknowledge mistakes made in their pursuit of better ways, the sooner those mistakes can be "cracked open," revealing the lessons they contain. Those lessons represent the next generation of better ways.

Confront

I have encouraged the creation of change-friendly cultures, ones in which people are encouraged to look for, consider, and try alternatives to the status quo—to make mistakes. I have suggested leadership behavior that doesn't punish people for making mistakes when trying new activities or techniques, but actually honors them for doing so. In such a culture, and in response to that type of leadership, people will try new things, make mistakes, and learn from those mistakes while progressively—and continuously—improving their performance and their productivity.

In almost every organization, there will be people who just won't "play." They will not participate in deliberation, they will not demonstrate good faith in their dealings with their leaders or with their peers, they will not participate actively the Relentless Search for Better Ways, and they will resist leaders' efforts to coach them. Some people are simply in the wrong place at the wrong time. They're working in a company where their leaders expect them to do things they're unwilling to do.

> **When, by their behavior, people demonstrate their inability or unwillingness to meet reasonable expectations, they create a situation that must be confronted. Enter the leader.**

Please note that what must be confronted in this scenario is behavior, not people. That is a key distinction. Failure to meet reasonable expectations is attributable to some combination of ability and willingness. As a facilitator, you must determine which is currently "in play" for underperformers.

After satisfying yourself that the person is able to perform up to your expectations, you can then determine if additional training is needed in order for them to know how to meet those expectations. If so, provide that training. But if, after concluding that ability is not the issue, you're left with that person's willingness—or, more accurately, that person's unwillingness. Whenever you reach that conclusion, I strongly encourage you to confront that unwillingness.

Here are some suggestions for conducting such a confrontation:

1. Explain that you are satisfied that the person has the ability to meet your expectations.

2. Explain that you are satisfied that the person understands how to meet your expectations.

3. Share the conclusion you've drawn, that the only reason the person is still not meeting your expectations is because he/she is unwilling to do so.

4. Ask the person to explain his or her unwillingness.

5. After asking for this explanation, be quiet and wait for the person to respond.

Can people change? Sure, they can, but some will not change without some encouragement in the form of confrontation and coaching. That requires leadership, leadership at the point of contact.

Leadership is not about hiring a team of perfect people. It's more a matter of developing the imperfect people you have.

> **Most people will respond favorably to effective leadership. Some won't, and you do a disservice to those who will by tolerating those who won't. So don't.**

Closing Thoughts on Leadership

Can you see how leadership is the common thread in all the topics we've covered so far? Organizational success does not just happen. Without effective leadership, the Happily Ever After myth will prevail, and the Relentless Search for Better Ways will never see the light of day. Without effective leadership, bad cultures will trump good initiatives. Without effective leadership, accountability will remain nothing more than a buzzword, while victimhood rules the day.

Leadership and accountability are inseparable. While they are always important, there are times and circumstances when they are, in fact, vitally important. When the status quo is working, when strategies, initiatives, and practices are producing great results and when people are working together with few conflicts, leaders' jobs are relatively easy.

But when the status quo begins to break down, when strategies fail, when initiatives fall flat or are stillborn, when the practices that once worked so well lose their effectiveness, and when people problems become the order of the day, leadership and accountability take on tremendous importance.

Let me leave you with this thought on these two requirements for organizational success:

LEADERSHIP & ACCOUNTABILITY
Most Difficult When They're Most Needed

Chapter 8 Summary

- Effective leaders facilitate crucial organizational processes.

- When functioning as facilitators, leaders directly impact organizational processes by addressing them indirectly.

- In order to produce benefits, initiatives must be executed. Without effective facilitation, execution won't happen.

- Translating strategic expectations into specific activities for people at operational levels is a crucial step in facilitating execution.

- Actionable plans must include specific *activities* to be performed by specific *people* within specific *timeframes*.

- I strongly encourage tactical leaders to employ a collaborative approach for translating strategic expectations into actionable plans.

- While their styles or approaches will vary, effective leaders facilitate the execution of initiatives and implementation of plans by providing appropriate, timely and relentless follow-up.

- What gets measured gets done. What doesn't get measured doesn't get done.

- When you see people trying something new or different, no matter how poorly they may be performing, celebrate their *effort*.

- Consoling people who are expressing appropriate, rational feelings about setbacks is something leaders can do to help those people get past the setbacks.

- Learning is one of the crucial processes that leaders facilitate. Setbacks provide excellent opportunities for them to do so.

- When, by their behavior, people demonstrate their inability or unwillingness to meet reasonable expectations, they create situations that must be confronted. Enter the leader.

- Most people will respond favorably to effective leadership. Some won't, and you do a disservice to those who will by tolerating those who won't. So don't!

- Leadership and accountability are most difficult when they're most needed.

CHAPTER 9

How Winning Occurs—in the Real World

One of the points I hope you've taken from this book so far is that organizational success—like individual success—is a process, not an event. In fact, it is a composite of several processes.

In this final chapter, I want to share some thoughts about how success is achieved, how winning occurs, in the real world. The processes that contribute to success often include alternatives to the things that have been done, the way those things have been done—and even alternatives to the way participants have *thought*. I would be remiss if I didn't include a preview of how you can expect all these changes to happen. As I take you through the characteristics of how most worthwhile changes are made, I invite you to reflect back on your own life experiences and think about the changes you've been able and willing to make.

Making Worthwhile Changes

Here are the four characteristics of how worthwhile changes are made, how organizational and individual success is achieved in the real world:

1. Progressively—important changes do not occur overnight
2. A little theory and a lot of effort—making changes requires more than just ideas
3. Some success and some failure—you'll most certainly encounter failures along the way
4. From the inside-out—staying the course and working through the failures requires mental, as well as physical, discipline

Progressively

Quick, how many substantive, worthwhile improvements in your life have been made overnight? Have you had many instant successes? Have you discovered any legitimate quick fixes or shortcuts to success? I'll go out on a limb here, and guess that your answer is no. And there's good reason—*there are none!* That's none, zip, nada.

> **Individual and organizational success is achieved over time, not overnight**

That being the case, there is a widely held delusion in our society that stands as a huge obstacle to success. That obstacle is our addiction to instant gratification. We want what we want, and we want it *now*. Worse, we not only want it now, we expect—*demand*—it now.

Having agreed that winning or success is a process, not an event, can you see how the addiction to instant gratification is the kiss of death for achieving that success? Those who embark on a process that can produce desirable results must continue with that process long enough for it to do so. But if they are so unrealistic as to expect immediate results, what would you expect them to do when those expectations aren't met? Does the word, "quit" come to mind? "We tried it and it didn't work" is an often-heard "mantra" for people who will only agree to try alternatives if they will produce better results immediately.

Compare that approach to what you've learned from your own experiences. Losing weight is something many people set out to do—several times in some cases. If you're one of those people, you've certainly found that promises of instant success notwithstanding, losing more than a pound or two takes sustained effort over a reasonable period of time. It just isn't going to happen overnight. If the focus and effort go away, the weight doesn't. If you set out on that process expecting instant, or even quick, results, and those results aren't forthcoming, your disappointment—in combination with the loud growling noise coming from your stomach—can lead you to the nearest fast-food place. Once there, you order everything on page two of the menu—and a diet drink.

So progressively means over time, a reasonable period of time, enough time for your process to gain some traction, build momentum, and start producing results.

> **Progressively also means that you must persevere beyond the point at which the new begins to wear off.**

You'll recall from our discussion of the Happily Ever After cycle (Chapter 2), that no matter how much initial enthusiasm we have for something that's new to us—in this case a new process—the "new" *always* wears off. Where processes for making worthwhile changes are concerned, the "new" will probably wear off *before* those processes produce many—or any—tangible results. In order to achieve those desired results, we'll have to stay the course.

Back to a real-world example, another that most of us are familiar with: physical fitness. Over the last decade, two things have been happening with us Americans and our physical condition. On one hand, we're being told that as a people, we are overweight and getting more so. On the other hand, there seems to be an ongoing "fitness craze." Don't ask me to explain how both could be happening at the same time, but since so many of us fall into one of those "camps," I'm covering them both. I've already alluded to the group looking to lose weight, so let me take a shot at the fitness faction.

Perseverance after the "new" wears off is one example of how processes pay off progressively. Does that apply to fitness? Do teenagers find their parents boring?

Let's say you're smitten with the desire to improve your fitness, and in your smitten state you purchase an exercise machine—a treadmill. You get it home, set it up, don your fitness costume and running shoes, strategically place a television set, bottles of water and towels, turn on the 'mill and climb aboard. There you are, embarked on the road to fitness. Your first session or two on your new treadmill go fine, and then a strange thing begins to happen. What was fun, exciting, exhilarating the first few times turns into drudgery—sweaty drudgery! The "new" has worn off, the thrill has gone, and suddenly there are dozens of other tasks that are far more important to you than spending time on the treadmill.

And how do scenarios such as this one play out? In consignment stores. That's right, consignment stores, places where, for a fee, the merchants will sell other people's stuff. Today, in just about any city of any size, there are consignment stores where you can buy used—that's *slightly* used—fitness equipment for a very good price.

Organizations are no strangers to this same phenomenon. The example that comes most readily to mind is something I've referred to as "initiative du jour." Too many organizational initiatives fail to produce the results for which they were designed. One reason for their failure is a lack of perseverance on the part of the people responsible for executing those initiatives. Leaders discontinue their facilitation, and people at the operational levels discontinue their implementation efforts before measurable results are achieved. The "new" wears off, efforts are curtailed, and the initiatives—along with their potential value—are discarded, to be replaced with yet another "initiative du jour."

> **In the real world, where we all live and work, success is a process, not an event. And success in the real world is achieved *progressively*.**

A Little Theory and a Lot of Effort

Our current Information Age could just as easily be dubbed the Theoretical Age. Much of the information being produced and disseminated is in the form of ideas, suggestions, and advice—theory. The same is true of the thousands of seminars, workshops, and conferences held every day. At least some of the sessions at these events are forums for learning, for improving skills and performance. For that matter, couldn't we put religious events in that same category? More on that later. There is certainly no shortage of theory in any area.

So what's wrong with theory, with ideas on making improvements in our lives? The short answer is nothing. The longer and more accurate answer is, "Nothing, as far as theory alone goes." The problem is, theory as a standalone just doesn't go anywhere. Somebody has to take it there, and that's called effort.

Again, I'll ask you to think back on the substantive improvements you've made in your life. Consider the relationship between theory—your ideas on what needed to change, and how to go about changing it—and the effort required to actually make those changes. Without the theory, you might not have gotten started. But without the effort, all the theories in the world would have yielded little in the way of progress.

> Individual and organizational underperformance can be attributed, at least in part, to the "love affair" so many people have with theory and their unwillingness to convert theory into action.

More accurately, it's probably not so much an aversion to effort as it is an aversion to the inevitable mistakes they expect to make when translating ideas into action.

In Chapters 6 and 7, I shared my Relentless Search for Better Ways model, a four-step process for seeking out, implementing, and fine-tuning alternatives to the status quo. The first step in that model, Deliberate, is done in support of the second step, Decide. As we all know from personal experience, many people deliberate in lieu of deciding. Fearing that they may make "bad" decisions—or maybe just fearing the prospect of making any decisions—they continue deliberating. They conduct more meetings, gather more data, form more committees. But what they don't ever seem to get around to doing is make decisions.

Our theory-to-practice phenomenon works in pretty much the same way. As a professional speaker and trainer, I've seen plenty of examples. Leadership and sales are two disciplines that offer an endless stream of theories. Books, tape programs, seminars, and workshops focusing on those two topics abound. Business owners, association executives, company presidents, and managers from all levels attend and send their employees to these events. And I believe that the information provided—the theories espoused—are, for the most part, sound. The people who participate in these events are exposed to ideas that could, *if* adapted and implemented, improve their processes and their results. Unfortunately, that's a pretty big "if."

Most of us are creatures of habit. We develop our routines, our processes, our mannerisms, and the things we do and how we do them. And after they're in place, it takes real commitment and effort to change them. Given our demand for instant gratification and our reluctance to abandon the familiar, comfortable status quo in favor of unfamiliar, uncomfortable alternatives, the "good ideas" we hear aren't always converted into effort—at least not sustained effort.

I mentioned leadership as a topic for which theories abound. The people who attend leadership conferences or participate in leadership training are, for the most part, people already in leadership positions. Some may be candidates for such positions, but all of them would profess their interest in learning how to improve their leadership skills.

Surely they will show up willing to consider—and ultimately try—alternatives that they believe will yield better results. Happily, many of them do. Others seem to lose interest when the theory being offered goes from the things they can expect from others, e.g., more active participation in the Relentless Search for Better Ways, to what *they* must do, e.g., facilitate, follow up, coach, and confront.

> Too many people in leadership positions seem to believe that theory, in the form of directives, policies, and employee training, is all they must provide in order to improve performance and productivity.

Facilitation and leadership—along with the mechanics of those roles—are nothing more than theories until someone does something with them. Attending conferences and successfully completing courses, while important, is simply not enough. Too much theory; too little effort.

Selling is the other profession that seems to attract a lot of attention from speakers, writers, trainers, and consultants. Like participants in leadership sessions, many sales professionals continuously tweak their selling skills. Others continue using the same techniques they adopted early in their careers, dismissing alternatives presented by speakers, trainers, consultants, sales managers, and peers as either something they "already do," something they "tried and it didn't work," or something that "wouldn't work with the people they call on or in the territories they work." They leave the theory in the classroom and cling tenaciously to the status quo.

Let me share one last example of how people satisfy themselves with exposure to theory while making little effort to implement it. I think I mentioned religion earlier, and I'd like to close this discussion of theory and effort by giving you an assignment. If you accept and complete it, you'll have had another graphic example of the gap between ideas and behavior. Here we go.

Here's a homework assignment. This coming Sunday, I'd like you to be an observer in a church parking lot—pick any church. On Sunday morning, I want you to get to that church parking lot a few minutes before the service concludes. Find a parking place as close as possible to the door people will use when the service is over. Roll down your windows, so you can hear what they say to the preacher or priest as they file out. Hearing what they say isn't absolutely essential, so if you can't park close enough to hear, just watch what the people do.

For the preceding hour or so, they have been engaged in spiritual or religious exercises that we can refer to as theory. The worship service itself is important, but the primary objective for attending such services is to learn, and commit or recommit to applying spiritual or religious principles in daily life, right?

So the service ends, and the participants file out past the cleric. If you're close enough, you might hear them say things like "wonderful service," "great message," or other professions of appreciation for what was said. But after they're past the preacher or priest and out in the parking lot, what happens to their pace? I think you'll see it quickening as they move to their vehicles. In a matter of minutes, vehicles are moving toward the parking lot exits. What would you say the drivers' primary objective is at this point? *To beat the members of other congregations to the cafeteria!* And what happens if one of these drivers cuts another off, fails to yield the right of way, or otherwise violates the other's "rules"? There may be both verbal and nonverbal reactions. My guess is neither will be consistent with the spiritual or religious theory that was covered in the recently completed service.

Finally, one might wonder what happened to the spiritual or religious theory. Some might conclude that it just "flew out the car window" when the other driver committed the indiscretion. But I offer a different conclusion: it never got in the car at all. It was left in the sanctuary, or wherever the service was conducted. The proof of people's spiritual or religious beliefs is not in how they behave in places of worship, but how they behave in parking lots, on the street, in their homes, and on their jobs—in every other forum in their real world.

> **Where individual and organizational success is concerned, it's not just ideas that matter, it's what people do with those ideas.**

A little bit of theory and a lot of effort will yield far better results than a whole lot of theory and no effort.

Some Success and Some Failure

Have I mentioned that setbacks are inevitable? People and organizations engaging in the Relentless Search for Better Ways will make far more mistakes than those who are less ambitious and less aggressive in their pursuit of process improvement. I'm convinced that one reason people are hesitant to convert theory into practice, to try new activities or new techniques, is because they know that their early efforts will be imperfect—even clumsy. In our society, we have been conditioned not to experiment, not to try alternatives, even when our activities and techniques lose their effectiveness. A harsh observation? You be the judge.
How would you finish this time-honored statement: "Anything worth doing is worth doing _____"?

Set aside the clever words you've heard used, the humorous innuendos, and reflect back on the words your parents, teachers, coaches—all the people who lined up to help you grow into a responsible member of society—would have used.

The most common responses people recall are "well" and "right," so the statement would read: "Anything worth doing is worth doing well or right".

Who could quarrel with that sentiment? We've heard it so many times that we accept it without reservation. It's a basic truth—or is it? What does it really mean, and how have we chosen to use it when making choices?

Before going any further, I want to offer an alternative to the old "anything worth doing…" saw. The fear of *not* doing something well or right can discourage people from trying alternatives to the status quo, and that will be the kiss of death for the Relentless Search for Better Ways. What I want you to be willing to do right now is consider the following alternative:

> **Anything worth doing
> is worth doing poorly**

How many of the tasks or activities that you perform well or right today are ones that you performed clumsily or poorly the first few times, maybe the first few dozen times, you tried them? My guess is that they number in the dozens, maybe even the hundreds. You began performing them with the expectation that some day you would perform them well or right, but your early efforts were neither, were they? So how did you get from "clumsily" or "poorly" to "well" or "right"? You had to practice. You had to give yourself permission to make mistakes, to endure mediocrity on your way to mastery. And it worked.

Individuals within organizations may have used that old "anything worth doing…" belief to avoid trying alternatives to tasks or techniques that they perform well or right, even if those tasks or techniques themselves don't work so well or right anymore. If there is no organizational tolerance for mediocre, clumsy, or poor initial efforts—or if people have convinced themselves that there is no such tolerance—don't look for them to embrace the Relentless Search for Better Ways. They may participate in the first two steps, Deliberate and Decide, but when it's time for the Implement step, they're nowhere to be found. If they believe their job security is threatened whenever they make mistakes—even mistakes made in a good-faith effort to improve performance—then they will avoid trying new things. And who could blame them?

This is yet another opportunity for leaders to facilitate change from the inside out. Part of creating a change-friendly culture is assuring people that not only will mediocre, clumsy, or poor initial efforts be tolerated; they will be acknowledged and honored when they're made in pursuit of better ways.

Here's an example that illustrates the relationship between leadership, a change-friendly culture, and people's willingness to try new things.

During their first two or three years of life, children are bombarded with new skills to learn. Hey, they're brand-new, and so are all the wonderful things they see tall people doing, like walking. Do you remember learning to walk? Probably not, but I'm sure you remember watching children learn this important life skill. How would you describe their first attempt? How about their first twenty attempts? I didn't ask about their first fifty, because kids are pretty quick learners. As I see it, there are several reasons for their rapid progress at learning some fairly difficult skills.

First, they're driven by some inner urge—they're relentless and almost fearless. Second, and here's where parents come into play, they seem to know that their "leaders" won't hold their mistakes against them. Based on the culture that parents create and sustain for them, they know that mistakes are not "bad." We not only allow our children to make mistakes, we encourage them to do so, and when they do, we praise them.

Can you see how the culture we create for our children is change-friendly? Children are encouraged to experiment, to take risks, to make mistakes, and to learn from them. So, who creates that culture, and how? It's the leaders—in this case, the parents.

Can you see how the people in that culture respond? Children try new things in the presence of the most important people in their lives, their parents. Inevitably, they make mistakes, again in front of their parents. And what do they do after their poor performances? They try again, and again, and again until they've converted their early mediocrity into performance that could be accurately described as doing something "well" or "right."

Continuous learning is more than just a good idea. In a world characterized by continuous change, continuous learning is a prerequisite for keeping up. Gaining and maintaining any sort of competitive edge requires an aggressive pursuit of alternatives, aka the Relentless Search for Better Ways. Before we can expect people to proactively pursue better ways, we must create cultures that not only spell that out as an expectation, but also support the people who look for and implement alternatives to the status quo.

Individual and organizational success doesn't just happen. It's a process characterized by trial and error. What that means is that, while you'll enjoy some successes along the way, you'll also encounter plenty of failures. Failure is an inherent part of success. It's not the failures that do us in; it's the choices we make about them:

> **Success and failure will characterize your efforts to achieve any worthwhile objective.
> Your commitment to achieving that objective is best measured by your responses to failures.**

From the Inside Out

The phrase "your responses to your failures" makes a great segue to this fourth characteristic of how success is achieved. It's not like experiencing failures along the way is just a possibility, or even a probability—it's a certainty. Failures come in all shapes and sizes, and in varying degrees of intensity. They often show up when we least expect them. Unpleasant surprises—unlike Happily Ever Afters—do "just happen."

Our commitment to achieving whatever it is we've set out to achieve is not tested or measured by our successes. It's the *failures* that reveal what's on the inside—the courage, faith, strength of convictions, passion, and perseverance necessary to transcend the failures and stay the course. Winning, like leadership, is an inside-out phenomenon.

Accountability is a recurring theme for me, and I've made many references to our choices and their consequences. The relationship between our physical choices—what we say or do—and their consequences is readily apparent. Less apparent, but far more powerful, is the relationship between our mental choices—our thoughts—and their consequences, our perceptions, feelings, and behavior.

In Chapter 2, we saw how the Happily Ever After myth is based on deeply held beliefs. Oh, they're mistaken beliefs, but they're no less powerful than they would be if they were valid. So we started by looking at something on the *inside* and worked our way *out* to consider activities and techniques for achieving success. And now we're returning to our starting place, and to what I see as the starting place for every step in whatever process we're implementing.

We always start with the mental choices we make, our thoughts. So I'll conclude this chapter—and this book—with yet another life experience, one that reinforced for me the power of mental choices.

The Morning After

When fighting night battles, the absence of light can work to the distinct disadvantage of a stationary unit being attacked. In my first encounter with enemy soldiers, my unit was stationary and under attack, and it was dark—real dark. The North Vietnamese knew exactly where we were, so the darkness worked to their advantage. To ensure that our defensive fire was targeted on them, we needed to be able to see them, so all night we were supported by artillery illumination rounds (flares) fired from a battery several miles away. The light from those rounds, being artificial and moving, gave the terrain and the people a surreal look that night. We were eager for the sun to rise. Fortunately, we were able to hold out until it did. Trust me, there were moments when the issue was in doubt.

Sunrise was welcome, and as the natural light replaced the eerie artificial illumination, we could see much more clearly. But with that clarity came a graphic vision of death and devastation. During the night's fighting, several Marines had been killed, and many more wounded. Our hilltop position had been bombarded with mortar rounds and swept by rocket-propelled grenades as well as machine-gun and small-arms fire. The initial volley had done most of the damage. In that volley, several Marines in my platoon had been wounded, one mortally. Ironically, the first Marine I lost was from my hometown.

After having held off the enemy assault, our first order of business that morning was to patrol the areas from which we had been attacked to ensure that the enemy had withdrawn, or to engage and destroy them, or force them to withdraw. As the only officer left standing, I was preparing to lead that patrol.

I had just experienced several "firsts": my first firefight, my first opportunity to command Marines in combat, and my first casualties—my first Marines killed in action. My adrenaline of the night before was pretty much gone, and I was struck by the enormity of what had happened, of the lives that had been lost. I was also engaged in some pretty intense scrutiny of my performance. I was doing a lot of second-guessing and going through some "what ifs."

Apparently, my facial expression and body language revealed my distracted state, and it was no source of comfort to one Marine who would be part of our morning patrol.

Here we were, preparing to search for the people who had spent the past several hours trying to kill us. To get to the tree line from which they had been firing, we would have to cross 200-300 meters of open ground, where we would be highly visible. Then, when we got to where they had been, there was a good chance that we'd have to fight them. Can you see how the Marines involved would want to have total confidence in the person leading them?

The mental processes I was going through—rehashing, second-guessing, and even grieving—were all perfectly normal. Under other circumstances, they would even have been good things to do. Under those circumstances, however, they were luxuries neither I nor the Marines on my patrol could afford.

As we were completing our preparations for the patrol, I was standing apart from the platoon, studying my map. A young Marine—a private first class—eased up beside me. He put his hand on my shoulder and brought me back, mentally, to where I had to be for him, and for all of us. He looked me in the eye, not in a challenging or confrontational way, but comfortingly, and said, "Lieutenant, it don't mean nothing. Let it go."

Do you think he was telling me that the casualties, the deaths we'd suffered, were meaningless? If that's what you think he meant, then you don't know much about Marines. On the contrary, he was telling me that unless I got my head in the game, put what had happened behind me, and provided the quality of leadership he and the other Marines had every right to expect, then more casualties could be expected. He was giving me the same advice I shared earlier in this book, something I referred to as an accountable choice after a setback. Remember? "Get over it and get on with it."

One phase of "getting over" setbacks, losses, or failures is to do some appropriate, rational grieving. "Appropriate" and "rational" relate to the intensity and duration of the grieving, with the understanding that some forms of grieving may be disproportionate to the gravity of the setback. "Appropriate" and "rational" also relate to the *circumstances* that prevail after the setback. In a combat situation, "appropriate" and "rational" are determined more by the circumstances than by the gravity of the setback.

The death and suffering of the night before certainly warranted some proportionate grieving, but the circumstances trumped the gravity. More than cursory, superficial grieving would have been inappropriate and irrational. The wisdom and courage of that young Marine helped me see and respond to the sad truth that under those circumstances, my grieving simply had to be postponed.

So what's my point? Quite simply, it is to remind you that the actions we take in response to setbacks in life have their origins in the mental choices we make *about* those setbacks. The quality of our behavior reflects the quality of our thoughts.

At every turn in this book, I've encouraged the development and practice of individual and organizational accountability. And now, at the end, I'm starting to understand that accountability isn't something we obtain or develop; it's something we already possess. Here's what we must understand about accountability:

> **Our challenge is to become more diligent, more consistent, in acknowledging our accountability and in thinking and behaving in ways that express it. We must also model it for others.**

Several years ago, I came up with something I call "the Rule." After completing this book, it has taken on a new, clearer meaning for me. So in closing this chapter, and this, my first book, I want to thank you for reading what I've been learning as I wrote. I leave you with the idea I'll use to begin my next book. I hope to encounter you again, in its pages.

THE RULE
Only You Can Choose the Quality of Your Days.

APPLICATION
To Have Exceptional Days,
Stop Looking For Exceptions to THE RULE!

Chapter 9 Summary

- Winning is a process, not an event.

- Individual and organizational success is achieved over time, not overnight.

- Winning requires perseverance beyond the point at which the new wears off.

- One explanation for individual and organizational underperformance is the "love affair" so many people seem to have with theory and their aversion to effort.

- Failure is an inherent part of success. It's not the failures that do us in; it's the choices we make about them.

- Success and failure will characterize your efforts to achieve any worthwhile objective. Your commitment to achieving that objective is best measured by your responses to your failures.

- Our challenge is to become more diligent, more consistent, in acknowledging our accountability and in thinking and behaving in ways that express it. We must also model it for others.

- THE RULE: Only you can choose the quality of your days.

- APPLICATION: To have exceptional days, stop looking for exceptions to THE RULE!

Acknowledgements

Writing and publishing a book, like so many other worthwhile ventures, is truly a "team sport." The list of people who have touched this project over the years is far too long to fit on these pages. I am indebted to all of you, and I want to express my heartfelt appreciation to the following "extra mile" contributors.

To Sally Rice Jones, who took on the task of translating "Texan" into readable English in her role as editor. Sally's command of the English Language is exceeded only by her patience and her intolerance for parenthetical phrases.

Bill Hyche, who helped shepherd us through the transition from writing to publishing. Call me impulsive, but when setting out to do something I've never done before, I like to get advice from people who have. Bill has, and his help early on got us headed in the right direction.

Debby Cole, a long-time client, friend and believer in my work drew "the short straw" on this project. Proofing a manuscript is a tedious, thankless task, especially when working under tight time constraints, and that's what we asked Debby to do. The excellent observations and recommendations she made have contributed to the quality of the finished product. They've also convinced me that Debby is the person to call on for all my future tedious, thankless tasks. How's that for something to look forward to, Deb?

Mike Dewey provided an always-interesting Aggie perspective

on the process. I'm not sure if it was his days playing football at Texas A&M, his experience starting and running several companies or the influence of his wife—another Barbara—but some combination of factors have made Mike a living example of "whatever it takes."

John Torr, whose attention to detail is now legendary, has provided outstanding editorial support of articles I've written. His help with the book was equally valuable, and much appreciated.

Alan Haley, who apparently lugged the manuscript with him as he criss-crossed the country, also offered up many helpful suggestions. Alan and I share many things in common, key among them the fact that we're both former Marines. The Brotherhood is alive and well, and I appreciate your help with my book. *Semper Fi*, brother.

Jill Brant surely destined for corporate stardom, provided the suggestions that helped me transform a manuscript into this book. Thank you, Jill, for your wisdom and for your willingness to share it.

Bruce, "Uncle Moose" Smith, corporate executive, marketing guru, champion of the self-employed and cigar aficionado, who has always been available to offer a real-world perspective on just about anything. Many hours and many Macanudos later, it's a book.

Kimberly Ford, and everyone at The Visibility Company, who have translated concepts and ideas into the cover design for my book.

Finally to Ryan, Annie and Jessie Bearden, for providing your old Dad with so many great story lines and for teaching me so many priceless lessons. Most of all, thank you for being the lights of my life, for your patience with my clumsy attempts to be as good a parent as you deserve—and for your unconditional love when I've fallen short of the mark. Hey, I'm trainable…